WHAT IS HINDUISM?

WHAT IS HINDUISM?

Radical new perspectives on the most ancient of religions

Acharya Peter Wilberg

New Yoga Publications
2009

This edition published 2010 by
New Yoga Publications, Whitstable, United Kingdom
an imprint of
New Gnosis Publications

British Library Cataloguing In Publication Data
A Record of this Publication is available
from the British Library

Printed and bound in England by Antony Rowe Ltd
Distributed by Gardners Books, Eastbourne, Sussex

Printed and bound in the United States of America by CreateSpace.com

ISBN 978-1-904519-15-7

CONTENTS

NOTE TO THE READER

This book, like all other **New Yoga Publications**, not only adds to but also draws from Acharya Peter Wilberg's entire corpus of essays and books on 'The Awareness Principle' and its practice – 'The New Yoga of Awareness'. Each book being a compendium of selected essays from this corpus, the reader is asked to bear in mind that some repetition of textual content - both within and across different books - has been unavoidable. It is hoped that this element of repetition will not be an annoyance to the reader but instead serve to reinforce his or her understanding of the many different threads and dimensions of Acharya's thought – theological, philosophical, psychological and political – weaving them together in the context of a new thematic focus and thus revealing their interconnections in a new light.

PREFACE

In this book I bring together a diverse selection of essays and citations aimed at offering new answers to the question 'What is Hinduism?' In doing so, I also offer an introduction to Hinduism from a number of radically new perspectives – historical and philosophical, economic and political, socialist and Marxist. Their common aim is to overcome the whole idea of Hinduism as just one major world 'faith' or ethnic-cultural 'identity' among others - but instead to reveal anew the universal truth and essence of Hinduism as the 'Eternal Truth' or *Sanatana Dharma*[1].

Drawing on the most refined and sophisticated expression of Hindu religious philosophy[2], I argue that at its heart is an understanding of the divine unlike that of all other religions – whether 'monotheistic', 'polytheistic' or 'pantheistic'. This is the understanding that God *is not a being* – either in the form of a single 'supreme being', a multiplicity of natural or divine beings, or a philosophical abstraction of 'pure being' - 'Being' with a capital 'B'. More to the point, God is not a being that happens to have or possess 'consciousness'.

God is not a being 'with' consciousness. *God is consciousness.* This is not a consciousness that is 'yours' or 'mine', but one that constitutes the very essence of the divine - being the ultimate or divine source of *all beings* – of

9

everything that 'is'. I term this consciousness 'pure awareness' – meaning subjectivity or awareness *as such* in contrast to anything we are aware of. This distinction is central to what I call 'The Awareness Principle', a radical neo-Hindu approach to religion, life and science whose first principle is that *awareness* as such (Sanskrit *chit*) cannot, *in principle,* be reduced to the *property or product* of any thing or being that we are conscious or aware 'of' - including the human body or brain.

Understanding the divine as a universal, absolute and supreme *awareness* – transcending and yet also immanent in all beings – has implications that transcend theology and subvert our current understanding of both 'science' and 'religion'. At the same time they are wholly congruent with the *Marxist* understanding that religious concepts of God as a supreme, all-ruling *being* or group of beings arose with the development of class society and *its* rulers. Similarly, modern scientific concepts of consciousness as a mysterious by-product of 'matter' arose with the development of an industrial society oriented to the production of material commodities 'possessing' a mysteriously invisible and immaterial property – an 'exchange value' or 'market value' quite independent of their tangible, material nature and 'use value'.

By recognising the inner unity of *Hindu* and *Marxist* perspectives we can see that the 'supreme being' worshipped as the 'God' of the Abrahamic faiths is in effect a divinisation of the human *ego* – seen at the same time as a divine 'superego' capable of ruling over a divided world of competing personal, corporate and national egos.

A central aim of this book therefore, is to overcome the false division or dualism between Marxism – still wholly misunderstood as a form of crude philosophical 'materialism' – and the religious essence of Hinduism. This false opposition is of no small relevance to the future of India itself in an age characterised by both the dominance and on-going crisis of global finance capitalism and *its* hidden religion — what Marx called "the monotheism of money". To bring this age and its 'monotheism' to an end, along with *its* countless idols and fetishes (for example in the form of pop idols, media celebrities and consumer commodities) requires a *socialist theology* of a sort which transcends the realm of theology as such – offering also radical new understandings of both science and society, politics and economics, history and philosophy. A major thesis of this book is that within the history and diverse forms and expressions of 'Hinduism' lie the seeds, not just of a new and *universal* religious philosophy or 'theosophy' but also a revolutionary new *theo-scientific, theo-political, theo-economic, theo-ecological* and *theo-socialist* world view. Only such a radically new socialist understanding of Hinduism can, in my view serve the duty or *dharma* of overcoming the monotheism of money and its religion – a superficial concept of knowledge in the form of technological 'science' and a cultural *polytheism* of the commodities it fetishises.

To summarise: in this book I present the 'Eternal Truth' (*Sanatana Dharma*) of Hindu religious philosophy as a recognition that the question of God's reality *is not* – as both 'believers' and 'non-believers' *would have us believe* – a question of the existence or non-existence of the sort of *supreme being* worshipped in the Abrahamic faiths. In place of the idea of God as a supreme being – one that merely 'has' or 'possesses' consciousness – the radical essence of Hinduism lies instead in the recognition that God *is* consciousness, not a *supreme being* but a *supreme awareness*.

To 'be' is to be *aware* of being. Awareness therefore - though *not itself* a being – is nevertheless the pre-condition for the existence or 'beingness' of all that is – all things and all beings. As such its ultimate and divine *reality* cannot be questioned. For all things and all beings – including both human beings and divine beings or 'gods' – are in essence but individualised shapes, patterns, portions or personifications of that ultimate, universal and supreme *awareness* which is the very essence of the divine.

Reality – truth – is therefore essentially *subjective* in nature - neither the result of a Big Bang, the work of some 'Big Being' nor the product of some *objective* 'energy', 'force' or 'quantum field' of the sort deified by both the official 'church' of modern science and New Age spiritual pseudo-science. That is why the 'Eternal Truth' of Hinduism needs no objective 'proof' – for it is the recognition of the subjective nature of both being (*sat*) and knowledge (*vidya*).

1. 'Hindu' is not a Vedic or Sanskrit word, and neither of course is the word 'religion'. The Sanskrit word *dharma* can mean 'law', 'duty', 'way', 'path', 'teaching', 'religion', 'the natural or divine order of things' or 'the underlying reality supporting all things' (from the Sanskrit root *dhr* – to hold, make firm or support). For the purposes of his book I translate the particular expression *Sanatana Dharma* as 'The Eternal Truth' - a translation in line with the Brahmana Upanishad:

"Verily, that which is Dharma is truth. Therefore they say of a man who speaks truth, 'He speaks the Dharma,' or of a man who speaks the Dharma, 'He speaks the Truth.' Verily, both these things are the same."

2. The schools of late Tantric and Advaitic philosophy known collectively as 'Kashmir Shaivism' and united by that supreme 10th century synthesist of Indian religious thought and practice: *Sri Acharya Abhinavagupta.*

ON THE PROFOUND RELEVANCE OF HINDUISM

… Indian wisdom is flowing back to Europe and will bring about a fundamental transformation in our knowledge and thinking.

Arthur Schopenhauer.

Devoid of intellectual discernment are those Europeans who want to convert and civilise the Hindus.

… to begin with we see that Europe [can only] reproduce what in India, under the people of thinkers, had already accomplished several thousand years ago as a commandment of thinking.

Friedrich Nietzsche

Our purpose will surely be served when the Indian world-view becomes known. It will make us aware that we, with our entire religious and philosophical thought, are caught in a colossal one-sidedness, and that there can be found yet a quite different way of grasping things than the one which Hegel has construed as the only possible and rational way.

Paul Deussen

Brahman … is not conceptual knowledge of Being, though wisdom about Being (SAT-VIDYA), or about Brahman as Being, is part of it. Brahman is SAT (Being), the ground of all that is, including my own being which is of the nature of sheer, pure CHIT ('awareness', of which 'knowing' is itself a derivative mode)… From the Rigveda to Aurobindo, the central Indian tradition has made the choice in favour of the primacy and priority of consciousness.

J.L.Mehta

We Westerners are about to arrive at the crossroads that the Indian thinkers had already reached about seven hundred years before the birth of Christ.

… the gods were never dethroned in India. They were not disintegrated and dissolved by criticism and natural science, as were the deities of the Greeks … The gods of Homer became laughable, and were … later regarded as incompatible with the more spiritual and ethical, later concepts of divinity … India, on the other hand, retained its anthropomorphic personifications … to assist the mind in its attempt to comprehend what was regarded as manifested through them … What is expressed through the personal masks was understood to transcend them, and yet the garb of the divine personae was never actually removed. By this tolerant, cherishing attitude a solution of the theological problem was attained that preserved the personal character of the divine powers for all the purposes of worship and daily life, while permitting an abstract, supreme and transcendental concept to dominate for the more lofty, supraritualistic stages of insight and speculation.

The identity of the hidden nature of the worshipper with the god worshipped is the first principle of the Tantric philosophy of devotion [Bhakti].

Heinrich Zimmer

Once upon a time a *sannyasin* entered the temple of Jagganath. As he looked at the holy image he debated with himself whether God had a form or was formless. He passed his staff from left to right to feel whether it touched the image. The staff touched nothing. He understood that there was no image before him; he concluded that God was formless. Next he passed the staff from right to left. It touched the image. He understood that God had form. Thus he understood that God has form and, again, is formless.

The Divine Mother revealed to me in the Kali temple that it was She who had become everything. She showed me that everything was full of Awareness. The image [Murti] was Awareness, the altar was Awareness, the water-vessels were Awareness, the door-sill was Awareness, the marble floor was Awareness – all was Awareness. I found everything inside the room soaked, as it were, in Bliss – the

Bliss of *Satchitananda* (Being-Awareness-Bliss). I saw a wicked man in front of the Kali temple; but in him I also saw the power of the Divine Mother vibrating.

Shri Ramakrishna

It is no secret that we in the West live in a time of spiritual crisis. Western civilization has been guided by Christianity. Now it appears that this period is drawing to a close. Both religious institutions and social structures are in disarray. A great many things that were considered basic assumptions of western thought are being challenged. The reality of the external world, the soul, the linear nature of time.

Stephen Cross

For those now disenchanted with industrialization and scientific materialism as well as pseudo-spirituality, India's ancient spiritual heritage provides a rich alternative. Eastern philosophy, and the devotional heart of India's Vedanta in particular, can fill the empty shopping bag of our Western accomplishments.

Swami B. V. Tripurari

In the history of the world, Hinduism is the only religion that exhibits a complete independence and freedom of the human mind, its full confidence in its own powers.

Hinduism is freedom, especially the freedom in thinking about God. In the search for the supernatural, it is like travelling in space without a boundary or barrier.

S. Radhakrishnan

It is not too much to say that the mind of the West with all its undoubted impulses towards the progress of humanity has never exhibited such an intense amount of intellectual force as is to be found in the religious speculations of India ...These have been the cradle of all Western speculations, and wherever the European mind has risen into heights of philosophy, it has done so because the Brahmin was the pioneer. There is no intellectual problem in the West which had not its earlier discussion in the East, and there is no modern solution of that problem which will not be found anticipated in the East.

Matheson

Recently, increasing numbers of Westerners in revolt against what they have found to be the shallow, gadget-dominated, spiritually empty civilization of the West have turned to "Hinduism" in search of greater meaning or purpose in life. There is no doubt that the great Hindu tradition offers profound spiritual insights, as well as techniques for attaining self-realization, detachment, and even ecstasy.

Beatrice Pitney Lamb

India indeed has a preciousness which a materialistic age is in danger of missing. Some day the fragrance of her thought will win the hearts of men. This grim chase after our own tails which marks the present age cannot continue for ever. The future contains a new human urge towards the real beauty and holiness of life. When it comes, India will be searched by loving eyes and defended by knightly hands.

W. J. Grant

Indian thought, with its usual profundity and avoidance of arbitrary divisions, regards Philosophy as religious and Religion as philosophical. The "liberty-loving nations of the West" have been in the past greatly, and still are to some extent, behind India in the matter of intellectual and religious freedom. As has been finely said in India, *Satyannasti para dharmah* ('There is no religion higher than Truth') and as the Vedas have proclaimed, 'Truth will conquer' (*satyam jayate*).

Hinduism may not be called a religion in the sense other religions are known. It is much more than a religion, it is a total way of life. Hinduism has no founder. Its authority is Eternal Truth. The cumulative record of metaphysical experimentation. Behind the lush tangle of religious imagery, is a clear structure of thought. Compared to the rugged originality of the Indian traditions, the language of

- In Hinduism, a 'guru' or teacher is needed to aid the individual in cultivating a direct experience of the divine and recovering a sense of union with it. The guru is not an evangelist or priest there to preach a gospel or faith.

- Hinduism does not see the world as something 'made' by a God but is understood as a creative *manifestation* of the Divine – in the same way that speech is a *manifestation* of meaning and not something 'made'.

- Since the entire *world* and everything in it is *itself* a sacred revelation of the Divine, its sacredness cannot be reduced to that of scripture - the revealed *word*.

- The Divine is understood as both transcendent and immanent in all things and all beings, the primordial womb of All That Is. Whilst it has both masculine and feminine aspects it ultimately *transcends* all identities – and with them all distinctions of gender, caste, ethnicity and regional culture.

- Hinduism is 'a-theistic' – but only in the strict sense of not being *theistic* – not identifying the Divine with a supreme God-Being.

- Instead of being *monotheistic*, Hinduism is *monistic* – recognising the Divine as a singular, absolute, unifying our own bodies - or even just our own heads. The first step we can take towards experiencing the Divine Awareness is to become constantly aware – not just with our eyes but with our body as a whole – of the space *surrounding our bodies*. In this way we learn to sense space itself as an open and unbounded field *of* awareness – not 'our' awareness, 'yours' or 'mine', but that awareness which is the Divine. If we can also feel the *insideness* of our own bodies as a hollow space - not just the insideness of our heads but that of our chest, belly and abdomen – then we can learn to sense that 'inner' space too as a space of awareness - one not in any way separate from the space around us.

We know that matter is composed mostly of empty space. Through the simple practice of identifying with the space within and around our bodies - and experiencing them as one – we begin to feel the very materiality of our bodies as something as much pervaded by pure awareness as it is by empty space. We cease then, to experience ourselves as contained within our own skins and merely looking out at things through the peepholes of our eyes. Instead we begin to sense the entire physical environment around us in space as our own *larger body* – part of the universal body of the Divine Awareness. We feel our own 'smaller' human body then, as just one body among others contained within this *larger awareness* which, as the very 'aether' of space, surrounds, embraces and pervades them today's philosophers concerned with being often sound a little contrived. Hindus have always been metaphysicians at heart. It is the underlying ideas, and not the images which count. As stated at the outset in the Rig Veda: "Truth is one, the wise call it by various names."

Sir John Woodroffe

Hinduism has proven much more open than any other religion to new ideas, scientific thought, and social experimentation. Many concepts like reincarnation, meditation, yoga and others have found worldwide acceptance. It would not be surprising to find Hinduism the dominant religion of the twenty-first century. It would be a religion that doctrinally is less clear-cut than mainstream Christianity, politically less determined than Islam, ethically less heroic than Buddhism, but it would offer something to everybody. It will appear idealistic to those who look for idealism, pragmatic to the pragmatists, spiritual to the seekers, sensual to the here-and-now generation. Hinduism, by virtue of its lack of an ideology and its reliance on intuition, will appear to be more plausible than those religions whose doctrinal positions petrified a thousand years ago.

Klaus L. Klostermaier

It is … the office of Asia to take up the work of human evolution when Europe comes to a standstill and loses itself in a clash of vain speculations, barren experiments and helpless struggles to avoid the consequences of her own mistakes. Such a time has now come in the world's history... the result ... will be no more Asiatic modification of Western modernism, but some great, new and original thing of the first importance to the future of human civilisation.

The later [Abrahamic] religions endeavour to fix the type of a supreme truth of conduct, erect a system and declare God's law through the mouth of an Avatar [God incarnate] or prophet ... The true divine law, unlike these mental counterfeits, cannot be a system of rigid ethical determinations that press into their cast-iron moulds all our life-movements.

The law divine is truth of life and truth of the spirit and must take up with a free living plasticity and inspire with the direct touch of its eternal light each step of our action and all the complexities of our life-issues. It must not act as a rule and formula but as an enveloping and penetrating conscious presence that determines all our thoughts, activities, feelings, impulsions of will by its infallible power and knowledge.

Only by our coming into constant touch with the Divine Consciousness and its absolute Truth can some form of the conscious Divine, the dynamic absolute, take up our earth-existence and transform its strife, stumbling, sufferings and falsities into an image of the Supreme Light, Power and Ananda [bliss].

... it is the individual who must climb to this state as a pioneer and precursor.

But if a collectivity or group could be formed of those who had reached the state of supramental perfection, there indeed some divine creation could take shape; a new earth could descend that would be a new heaven, a world of supramental light could be created here amidst the receding darkness of this terrestrial ignorance.

Sri Aurobindo

SAYINGS FROM THE HINDU KASHMIRI SAGES

Awareness is nature of the Self.

Awareness, Shiva, is the soul of the world.

Thus identifying with the universal awareness and attaining divine bliss, from where or from whom should one get scared?

For the yogi who has attained the state of Bhairava [simultaneous awareness of their outer and inner experiencing] the entire world [outer as well as inner] is experienced as their body.

from the Shiva Sutras of Vasugupta

The entire world is the play of the universal awareness.

One who sees it in this way becomes liberated while in the body.

Meditate on one's own body as the universe, and as having the nature of awareness.

The yogi is always mindful of that witnessing awareness which alone is the subject of everything, which is always a subject and never an object.

Whether outside or inside, Shiva [pure awareness] is omnipresent.

The yogi should contemplate the entirety of open space (or sky) as the essence of Bhairava [Shiva].

Meditate on space as omnipresent and free of all limitations.

Meditate on the skin as being like an outer wall with nothing within it.

Meditate on the spatial vacuity in one's body extending [outwardly] in all directions of space simultaneously.

Meditate on vacuous space above and vacuous space below.

Meditate on the body's matter as pervaded with space.

Meditate on one's own self as a vast unlimited expanse.

from The Vijnanabhairava Tantra

One should, setting aside identification with one's own body, contemplate that the same awareness is present in other bodies than one's own.

He whose awareness together with the other senses is merged in the interior space of the heart, who has entered into the two bowls of the heart lotus [diaphragm], who has excluded everything else from consciousness, acquires the highest fortune, oh beautiful one.

Shiva is the Self shining in all things, all-pervasive, all quiescent Awareness.

May the Shiva in-penetrated into my limited self through his power, offer worship to the Shiva of the expansive Self – the concealer of himself by himself!

Sri Somananda

Having made itself manifest, awareness abides as both the inner and the outer.

The visible world is the body.

Sri Utpaladeva

Immersing himself in the supreme reality, clearly aware that awareness is in all things, [the Yogi's] awareness vibrates. This throbbing pulsation [Spanda] is the Great Pervasion [Mahavyapti].

Every appearance owes its existence to the light of awareness.

Nothing can have its own being without the light of awareness.

Sri Kshemaraja

... the being of all things that are recognized in awareness in turn depends on awareness.

... the power of space is inherent in the soul as true subjectivity, which is at once empty of objects and which also provides a place in which objects may be known.

The Shastras [teachings] and Agamas [scriptures] proclaim with reasoned argument that it [awareness] is free of thought-constructs and precedes all mental representation of any objects.

Just as a man who has been ill for a long time forgets his past pain completely when he regains his health, absorbed as he is in the ease of his present condition, so too are those who are grounded in pure awareness free of thought-constructs no longer conscious of their previous [fettered] state.

The yogi should abide firmly fixed in his own nature by the power of expanding awareness ... relishing the objects of sense that spontaneously appear before him.

Bhairava [Shiva] is he whose light shines in the minds of those yogis who are intent on assimilating time into the eternal present of awareness.

The Power that resides in the
Heart of Awareness is Freedom itself.

Sri Abhinavagupta

FROM ATHEISM TO 'NOOTHEISM'

Hinduism is not reducible to any form of polytheism or monotheism. Instead it is essentially *monistic* – asserting the divinity and unity of a single divine reality – awareness – in all its multiple worldly manifestations and godly personifications. By recognising the divinity of this ultimate and universal awareness it is essentially 'nootheistic' - from the Greek *noos* – awareness.

- **Atheism**, strictly speaking, is not disbelief in God. It is disbelief in the existence of God as a BEING.

- **Theism** is the belief that God exists as a BEING.

- **Monotheism** is the belief that God is ONE supreme BEING separate from the world and other BEINGS.

- **Polytheism** is the belief in a plurality of Gods, each of which is a divine or trans-human BEING.

- **Hentheism** (from the Greek 'hen' meaning 'one') is the belief that God is the ONENESS of all beings or 'BEING' as such.

- **Henotheism** is a form of polytheism resting on the belief in one supreme BEING or God ruling over all lesser gods and beings, and regarded as 'god of gods'.

- **Pantheism** (from the Greek word 'pan' meaning 'all') is the belief that God IS the world – is ALL BEINGS.

- **Panatheism** ('Buddhism') is the belief that NO BEINGS exist, because everything is in a constant state of BECOMING.

- **Panentheism** (from the Greek words 'pan' and 'en', meaning 'all' and 'in') is the belief that all BEINGS dwell IN God, and that God dwells IN all BEINGS.

- **Nootheism** (from the Greek *noos* - 'awareness') is a form of 'panentheism' that identifies God with that absolute and divine Awareness from and within which all BEINGS constantly 'BE-COME' or 'COME-TO-BE'.

HINDUISM IN DISTINCTION
TO THE ABRAHAMIC FAITHS

'Hinduism' is a modern word for the world's oldest and still third-largest religion, with around one billion followers. And yet it differs from all of the 'Abrahamic' faiths – Judaism, Christianity and Islam – in the most fundamental of ways. Otherwise known as *Sanatana Dharma* ('the Eternal Truth') 'Hinduism' is not an ethnically exclusive religion and it understands itself as inclusively embracing the partial truths of other religions from within a higher, holistic perspective. In contrast, Judaism is both an ethnically and doctrinally exclusive religion, whereas Christianity and Islam are ethnically inclusive but doctrinally exclusive faiths.

The Persian term *Hindu* derives from the name of the *Sindhu* river – the Indus. And indeed the best symbol of Hinduism is a flowing *river* with many tributaries. Hinduism is not a monolithic 'faith' so much as an evolving and creative confluence of numerous diverse but non-dogmatic and non-exclusive religious world-views and philosophies rooted in the Indian sub-continent – in particular the Vedic and Indus Valley civilisations. For even the earliest 'Hindu' scriptures – the Vedas – recognised 'no religion higher than truth', holding truth as their most sacred religious value. In search of ultimate truths the countless religious and philosophical currents that have flowed from or into the fertile river that is 'Hinduism' have never been driven by institutional or scholastic disputes over questions of belief or basic 'credo'. For whilst 'faith' is merely 'believing' something to be true, truth itself is *knowing* it to be so. It is important to recognise that Hindu theology does not assume, like most Western philosophies and faiths, that 'truth' is a property of religious or scientific assertions or propositions 'about' reality. For even to assert or deny the mere existence of any thing or being - including a supreme being - assumes a prior *awareness* of that thing or being. From this it follows that the ultimate nature of truth can be nothing but *awareness* as such - understood as an ultimate or divine *knowing* - and not any thing or being that is known.

BASIC AND DISTINCTIVE ELEMENTS
OF THE HINDU WORLD-VIEW:

- In contrast to the Torah, Bible and Koran, Hindu 'scripture' has no dogmatically restricted canon of scriptures, no supreme institution, no single spiritual founder such as an Abraham, Moses, Jesus, Buddha or Mohammed and no authoritative leader such as a Pope, Archbishop, Ayatollah or Dalai Lama.

- Hindu scripture is not reducible to the principal Vedas ('the Knowledge'), but embraces a vast and diverse historical body of still-evolving spiritual teachings.

- God is not seen as a *person* or even a supreme being. Instead the Hindu gods in all their multiple forms are understood as diverse *personifications* of the Divine.

- Similarly, all individual beings are individualisations of the Divine. Thus the true Self (Atman) of every being is understood as both eternal and one with the Divine.

- Though not understanding God *as* a person, Hinduism not only allows for but encourages the attainment of a direct personal experience of the Divine – in particular through devotion to a chosen divinity or personification of the Divine.

- Hinduism stresses that the Divine needs to be *experienced* in order to be spoken of truly – simply citing or interpreting scriptures is no substitute for revelation emerging from direct experience.

- Strictly speaking, Hinduism is not a 'faith' at all – for faith is only needed where direct knowing (jnanas/gnosis) is lacking.

reality underlying All That Is – as a singularity or One-ness as such – not a single or 'One' God.

- The ultimate, absolute reality that is the Divine is traditionally called 'Brahman'. Brahman in turn may be called by the same name as many specific Hindu divinities such as Shiva, Vishnu, Kali etc. In this way, Hinduism affirms the unity of the gods and God, of diverse divinities and the singularity of the Divine.

- The essential nature of the Divine as a singular reality is understood through the Sanskrit term 'Sat-Chit-Ananda' ('Being-Consciousness-Bliss'). All of the many schools of Hindu religious philosophy ultimately address the question of how the meaning and reality behind this term can be understood and directly experienced.

- Hindu thought does not separate 'philosophy', 'theology', 'spirituality' and 'science' but is essentially 'theo-sophical' and 'spiritual-scientific' in character. 'Yoga' is the practical science of Hindu 'theo-sophy', aimed at cultivating and recovering knowledge and direct experience of the Divine in oneself and all things.

- So-called 'idol worship' is an important and powerful aspect of Hindu religious practice, but is not unique to it. The Abrahamic faiths idolise everything from sacred books such as the Torah, Bible or Koran to human beings such as Moses, Jesus or Mohammed – as well as worshipping before icons such as the cross or the crucified Christ. And today's secular culture is almost defined by its worship of 'pop' or 'celebrity' idols – and by the idolisation of the latest hi-tech commodities. For a Hindu, on the other hand, the essence of a religious idol is not any image, person or material 'thing' but rather the divine consciousness ensouling it – and ensouling all things. Both Judaism and Islam forbid the representation of God in the form of an image or object. Yet a Hindu idol is precisely not the 'representation' of a divine being or divine person all - but is instead the image, embodiment or personification of a state of divine consciousness.

- Since Hinduism not only recognises the universal nature of the Divine but also the reality of reincarnation, being Hindu does not depend on upbringing or ethnicity but on acceptance, experience and active embodiment of its religious world-view.

- The aim of the Hindu is both to enjoy this life, and to achieve liberation (Moksha) within it, overcoming the need for further physical incarnations.

WHAT HAS 'HINDUISM' TO SAY TODAY?

What has Hinduism to say today - to today's world?

What have its ancient and profound 'theo-sophical' traditions, uniting theology and philosophy, religion and science, psychology and metaphysics, to offer the world today?

As Gandhi said: "An eye for an eye makes the whole world blind." That is one major reason why a new and truly global 'Hinduism', one freed of attachment to ethnicity, caste and gender discrimination, communalism - and the current encroachments of global capitalism and consumerism in its mother country – is so much needed. Such a Hinduism would no longer be identical with 'India' or the ethnic Hindu Diaspora from the Asian subcontinent. Yet it alone could offer the world an alternative to the world-destructive war that is raging between:

1. rampant secular materialism, consumerism and imperialism,
2. its religious-political prop in the form of Judaeo-Christian Zio-Nazism, and
3. reactionary feudalistic and fundamentalist Islamism.

That is because the Hindu theosophical tradition offers us a fundamentally different understanding of both God and the Universe from that of both religious and scientific *fundamentalisms* – whether the fundamentalist dogmas of modern science and cosmology or those of the Abrahamic religions (Judaism, Christianity and Islam).

The difference is profound. For in the Hindu theosophical traditions of *Advaita* and *Tantra*, 'God' is *not* understood as some supreme being 'ruling' like a judge or politician over Creation and over Creatures of its own artificial 'making'. Instead God is understood as identical with *consciousness* – not individual consciousness but a Universal Consciousness out of which the entire universe, all of creation and all creatures emerge as through a process of spontaneous creativity. 'God', in this tradition, is not merely one being among others 'with' its own individual consciousness. Instead God *is* this Universal Consciousness out of which the entire universe emerges.

The entire universe of 'matter' is but a materialisation of this Universal Consciousness, emerging from its maternal womb or 'matrix' – and *not* the other way round as 'materialist' or even quantum-physical 'energeticist' science has it. For awareness *as such* cannot, *in principle*, be the by-product or property of any force, energy or material body we are *aware of* - including the human body and brain. It cannot - in principle – be a *property* of matter, energy or of any thing or *being* whatsoever – human or divine. For the Divine is not a being or Being, but the source of all beings – their primordial *awareness* of Being.

The Divine is a Universal Consciousness that has the character of an infinite field — not of 'energy', but of pure *awareness*. This is awareness inseparable and yet absolutely distinct from any content of consciousness – any thing we are conscious or aware *of*. Since it transcends every element of our conscious experience – every thing we can possibly be conscious or aware *of* – this pure awareness can also free us from *attachment* to all the things and activities that our everyday consciousness ordinarily binds us to.

Instead, things and all beings are individualised portions of this Universal Consciousness that *is* God, an infinite field of pure awareness that embraces and "enowns" them all. To *experience* this Universal Consciousness or pure awareness therefore, *is* to experience 'God' – the Divine. Yet this is no *impersonal* experience, impersonal consciousness or impersonal 'God'. How could it be, since it is the very source of our own personhood, individual consciousness – and that of all beings and all things?

In the Hindu Tantric tradition known as Kashmir Shaivism or 'Shiva-ism', God is not seen as a *person* like Christ or Krishna, nor as three persons or three persons in one. Yet neither is God an impersonal abstraction – but rather that Divine Universal Awareness which knowingly *personifies* itself in all persons. The word 'person' refers to a 'face' or 'mask' (*persona*). The image or *Murti* of the Hindu god *Shiva* is a symbol of the human face or *personification* of divinity. And it is the *Mantra* of *Shiva* that allows the Divine Universal Consciousness to 'per-sonify' itself in another way – to 'sound through' human beings (*per-sonare*).

Shiva, as *Mahadeva* or 'Great God', is always portrayed in a state of profound meditation. Who or what then, is *Shiva* meditating? He is meditating the Divine Universal Consciousness that is the very *source* of his own human image and form – and that of all beings, human and trans-human. That source is His Other – none other than the 'Divine Mother' – the 'Great Goddess' or *Mahadevi*. She is the 'pregnant' dimension of the Divine Universal Consciousness – its nature as dark, maternal womb and seed repository of all possible worlds and beings, and their power or *Shakti* of self-actualization and manifestation. *Shiva* on the other hand, is the Divine Universal Consciousness as the pure light of awareness – that which releases all potential worlds and beings into actuality or Being from the womb of potentiality or Non-Being.

In Tantric theosophy 'God' is the Divine Universal Consciousness (*Anuttara*) understood as an inseparable and dynamic relation of the divine-masculine (Shiva as *pure awareness* of all that manifests) and the divine feminine (*Shakti* as *pure power* of manifestation). This is God as *Shiva-Shakti*.

"Only a god can save us now." *Martin Heidegger*

Hinduism has no religious prophets, popes or 'saviours'. Yet *Shiva* is that most primordial 'god' who alone can "save us now" – saving us as individuals from descending with the world into violence and barbarism, offering us the freedom from bondage to the world that only a higher and deeper *awareness* can bring, and providing us with a gateway to the Great Goddess and to 'God' as such, experienced and understood not just as *Shiva* but as *Shiva-Shakti.*

Along with pre-historic mother goddesses or *Mahadevis, Mahadeva Shiva* is one of the oldest and most primordial of human god images. Yet the earliest and most primordial of gods are not merely those furthest behind us – and thus long since 'past' or 'transcended' by later, more historically recent gods. On the contrary, as Heidegger recognized, the earliest and most primordial god is the one who, having set out longest ago, is also *latest to arrive* – the last to fully realise itself and be recognized and understood *as* a god.

What Heidegger called "The Last God" – that god who will be *last to arrive* and is therefore *still to come* – that god is *Shiva. Shiva* is a god of the future and not merely the past, a god still to be fully born – not as a supreme God-Being nor as a supreme human Guru, Saviour or *Avatar* – but as a higher *Awareness.* To take *Shiva* into our hearts as our *personal* God or Divinity is to take the Awareness that he is as Supreme or Divine Guru – and as our personal mediator and gateway to the power or *Shakti* of that *trans-personal* awareness that is Divinity or 'God' as such. Human beings become Gurus not by virtue of being *sole* human embodiments of God (for there is no one who is *not* a living embodiment or 'son' or 'daughter' of God) but because they recognise *Shiva* alone – and *no human being or teacher* – as Supreme Guru. It is because of this that they are able to receive knowledge and enlightenment through Him, as well as from those higher, trans-human beings that dwell in His realm - that plane of awareness known as *Shivaloka*.

No world 'religion' is merely founded on a creed, faith, dogma or doctrine. Instead it is more like a great work of *drama* enacted on the stage of our earthly human reality - one designed to alter our metaphysical understanding and experience of ourselves and the world in the most direct way, and in doing so transform our way of being in the world and relating to others. It is because of their nature as religious dramas, that religions require characters – *dramatis personae*. Yet though these may draw from religious symbols of the past, if these symbols are imbued with new experiential and metaphysical comprehensions they become vehicles by which the *future* can realise itself in and transform the present.

A genuinely new future for humanity cannot be forged by clinging to the *past* and yet, in Heidegger's words, it is the "arrival of what has been" – of what has yet to be fully comprehended, experienced and *brought to presence in awareness*. The work of bringing to presence in awareness belongs to those few human beings whose awareness has already been expanded enough to receive currents of knowing that flow towards us from the future – and that also come down to us directly from the multidimensional universe of awareness surrounding us and the trans-human beings or 'gods' that dwell therein.

For the religious practitioner of Hindu Tantrism, to 'worship' a god is to *become* that god. This means to experience it directly - through our *body* and *as* our most essential *self*. This is not a self that 'has' or 'possesses' awareness but that Self which – like God – *is* awareness – an awareness infinite and unbounded, pervading not only our bodies but all bodies, and all of space and time. Shiva is 'Lord' because he is 'Lord of Yoga' – of meditation. The human image of *Shiva* presents him as *meditating* both himself and all things as an expression of the Divine - and therefore knowing himself as identical *with* the Divine. That is why the activity of meditating Lord Shiva meditating *his* Divine nature turns his *Mantra* and *Murti* into both a *personification* of our own Divine nature and a living personification *of* the Divine.

Knowing himself *as* the Divine through meditating his Divine Nature in human form, the image of *Shiva* reveals him to us not just as a 'symbol' of the divine but as a living embodiment of it – one that does not just teach us to meditate the Divine, but allows us to directly experience and identify with it in its most tangible, bodily and sensuous immediacy. Like *Shiva*, each of us can learn to wordlessly know and say – in and through every atom and cell of our body, every aspect of our self, and every element of our experience, that 'Shiva am I' (*Shivoham*) and that every 'thing' around us is a mere outward 'mark' or 'symbol' of Shiva - his *Lingam*.

Lingam means 'mark' or 'symbol'. The *Lingam* of *Shiva* is the *absolute symbol* of that absolutely pure and *symbol-free awareness* that *is* the Divine Universal Consciousness, and beyond which there is 'nothing higher' (*A-nuttara*). Only a new and invigorated Tantric Hinduism – and not any copycat form of narrow Indian religious nationalism and Hindu 'fundamentalism' – can bring human beings to the threshold of a *higher awareness* out of which alone the world can be transformed. We stand therefore at the dawn of a glorious *new* religious drama rooted in Hinduism – one that has the power to transform our world through *awareness* rather than war, and in doing so also undo the untold damage wrought by wars present and past. For before its occupation by Muslim invaders, even the land of Afghanistan, now but a ravaged site of global strife between Islamism and US Imperialism, was replete with temples celebrating *Shiva* and *Shakti* – in peace.

Yet what about Buddhism? The great religious drama that was seeded by the life of Gautama Buddha and the whole subsequent evolution of 'Buddhism' in all its stages can be seen as a first attempt to give birth to a 'new' Hinduism freed of ethnic, racial and caste distinctions – and freed also of crude 'theistic' understandings of God as a single being and of the Universe as a mere multiplicity of self-subsistent things. Yet like the birth of a universalist Christianity from an ethnically rooted Judaism, the 'birth' of Buddhism from 'Hinduism' - from Indian Vedic and Brahmanic culture — also ended up as a *miscarriage*. Put simply, Buddhism threw out the baby of true religious feeling and connection with the Divine with the bathwater of crude 'theistic' understandings *of* the Divine – whether 'monotheistic' or 'polytheistic'.

Instead of acknowledging the Divine as an Awareness with both a wholly trans-personal and transcendental nature *and* a personal face and faces, Buddhist philosophy sought to do away with the whole idea of beings, whether human beings or gods. Doing so however, it found itself forced to eventually replace them with numberless 'Buddhas' – each with their own highly individual character and qualities of awareness! Yet in place of the Divine Universal Awareness – itself 'no-thing' – it substituted the idea of a Nothingness that was not only empty of all things, but also empty of *awareness*.

The Buddhist idea of 'enlightenment' as 'becoming aware of' or 'awakening' to this *Absolute Emptiness* replaced the Hindu Tantric aim of experiencing this apparent 'emptiness' as the pure space (*Akasha*) and light (*Prakasha*) of an *Absolute Awareness* - one distinct from each and every thing we are or could be *aware of*. In this way the whole notion of *En-Lightenment* was divorced from the *Light of Awareness* associated with *Shiva* and with all those who shine with that Light – 'shining ones' being the root Sanskrit meaning of *Devas* or 'gods'. Buddhist spiritual *a-theism* then, replaced not just religious monotheism, polytheism, pantheism and 'panentheism' (the immanence of God in all things) but also Hindu Shaivist and Tantric 'nootheism' – the recognition that Awareness absolute and unbounded (Greek *noos*) *is* the Divine, personified as Lord Shiva. As a result the defining Buddhist principle of 'Awakening' (*Bodhi*) replaced the Tantric principle of Awareness (*Chit*). Hence all talk of 'Buddhist Tantra' is inherently misleading. For all the truly 'Tantric' elements of Buddhism derive from 'Hindu' Tantrism and not from Buddhism as such – from the religious principle and practice of 're-linking' to an *ultimate and divine awareness* and not from the secular principle and practice of seeking an *ultimate state of human awakening or enlightenment.*

How then can each of us actually begin to experience the reality of the Divine as Awareness? Normally we think of and feel our awareness as something contained within

all. We no longer see things or people merely as bodies 'in' space. Instead we sense both our own bodies and those of all the things and people around us as *living embodiments and expressions* of the pure awareness (*Shiva*) that permeates space, and of the innate vitality or *Shakti* that pervades it – the breath or 'air of awareness' that is called *Prana*. All this was already indicated in the *Vijnanabhairavatantra* - one of the most important practical treatises or *tantras* of Shaivist Tantra, and one of the many gifts of 'Hinduism' – more properly speaking the *Sanatana Dharma* or 'Eternal Truth'.

ON THE WONDERS OF
HINDU 'IDOL WORSHIP'

The belief that an image, icon or idol is a cruder, more naive or 'primitive' object of religious reverence or worship – or even an unholy object – is itself as crude as the belief that painting, sculpture and music are cruder or more 'primitive' mediums of expression of spiritual truth than the written or spoken word. In reality they can be wondrous mediums. As for the attack on idol worship by the Abrahamic faiths – Judaism, Christianity and Islam – this is nothing if not hypocritical. For not only do they have their own idols – the Christian crucifix or the Muslim Kaaba for example. They also revere their own holy books as sacred *objects* in themselves – not only decorating them or filling them with iconic images but going so far as to effectively elevate them to the status of religious 'idols'. Thus in Jewish religious practice, the holy scroll of the Torah is consecrated, housed in a sacred chamber, veiled and unveiled, carried round in procession, its tassels kissed etc.

What distinguishes the Abrahamic faiths from Hinduism and other 'Dharmic' religions such as Buddhism, Jainism and Sikhism, is not their rejection of idol worship as such therefore, but rather their exclusive iconisation and idolisation of *the word* – not least in its concrete, material manifestation as the stone tablets of Moses. The idolisation of a Holy Book is a recognition of the truth that it is more than a material artefact of paper and ink. Similarly however, there is more to a temple, cathedra, synagogue or mosque than brick or stone, more to music than man-made material instruments and the sound vibrations they produce, just as there is more to a painting than its pigments, more to a great religious sculpture or 'idol' than wood, stone or bronze or some idle fancy of the sculptor. That is why, in the Hindu tradition, worship of sculpted idols (Pratima) is no mere religious prop for the illiterate, the ignorant or the spiritual neophyte, even though there may be some who consider it so. For as Swami Sivananda writes:

"[Only] a pseudo-Vedantin ... feels that his Advaita [non-duality with the divine] will evaporate if he prostrates [before an idol]. Study the lives of the Tamil Saints ... They had the highest Advaitic realisation. They saw Lord Shiva everywhere, and yet they ... prostrated before the idol and sang hymns ... The idol in the temple was all Chaitanya or consciousness for them. It was not a mere block of stone."

And yet there *are* indeed sacrilegious forms of idolatry - two of which in particular dominate today's world. One is the 'bibliolatry' of literalist religious fundamentalisms – which take the words of their sacred texts literally, never going beyond their 'letter' to their many-layered meanings or polysemous 'spirit'. This is like mistaking the menu with the meal. The other form of sacrilegious idolatry is what

Marx called "the fetishism of the commodity" and "the monotheism of money" – in other words the religion of consumerism, which makes idols of branded products and uses glossy media icons to promote their worship. An advertising mantra such as "Real chocolate. Real feeling" says it all – showing how manufacturers seek an almost religious feeling of devotion to their brands and iconic logos by a purely artificial association with the entire range of authentic human feelings and values, from love to spirituality - even worship itself.* Just as Hinduism offers an alternative to the global disarray and conflicts brought about by the Abrahamic religions, so does genuine religious idol worship offer an alternative to - and a powerful weapon against - the religious fetishism, idolisation, and pseudo-spiritualisation of crass material commodities, whether chocolate, skin creams or cars. Even religious icons and idols are today reduced to the status of mere decorative items, whether sacred African carvings or statues of Buddha on the suburban mantelpiece of the bourgeoisie.

The term for 'idol worship' in Sanskrit – *murti darshan* – actually means simply 'image seeing'. Specifically it refers to seeing an image of the divine in the form of a god - whether through a 'vision' obtained in a dream or altered state of consciousness or in the form of a specially created religious picture, symbol or sculpture. From a Hindu perspective, meditation on the *form* of such an image or *murti* no more negates the acknowledgement of God's *formless* or invisible dimension than does carrying round and studying an artefact of paper and ink in the form of a Holy Book such as the Bible or Koran. On the contrary, precisely by virtue of its tangible, material form, the *murti* makes it easier to experience the omnipresence of the divine in all things, to understand that things are just as much symbols of the divine as words are, and to come to a direct experience of things (and not just the words with which we name them) as the manifest word of the divine, its material metaphors, its solidified speech. The *murti* does not hinder but offers a far more direct route to a living experience of the essence of the divine, revealing it as something neither formless and immaterial nor reducible to a particular form, but rather as a dynamic relation between formlessness and form - in tantric terms, the relation between pure awareness (Shiva) and its innate power (Shakti) of formative activity and material manifestation.

The multiplicity of human forms taken by images and statues of the Hindu gods does not imply any sort of 'anthropomorphic' idea of God of the sort that belongs exclusively to the Abrahamic religions – with their emphatic claim that Man was indeed made "in the image of God". In contrast, the human form given to images of the Hindu gods is designed to awaken the worshipper's experience of their own human bodily form as a fleshly embodiment and expression of 'spirit' – of that higher 'air' or 'aether' of awareness (*akash*) that ensouls all bodies as their vital breath (*prana*) and from which matter itself is formed. This aether may be perceived only as the seemingly empty space 'in' which the Murti stands as a mere object. In reality space itself (*kha*) pervades every object in it, just as it itself is pervaded by the aether of which all objects are formed. As the physicist Paul Dirac noted: "A place is nothing; nor even space, unless at its heart – a figure stands." The sacredness of the space in which the *murti* stands is both distinct and inseparable from it. It is what allows the *murti* to stand out or 'ex-ist' in its sacrality, just as it is the presence of the Murti that makes the space around it sacred, offering an experience of the divine aether of awareness (*akash*) surrounding and pervading it.

Yet just as a spiritual text or scripture may in itself be more or less superficial or deep in meaning, and the 'letter' of its word a more or less distorted human expression or translation of its wordless inner meaning or 'spirit' — so too can a *murti* be more or less crudely or beautifully crafted as an expression of spiritual truth. It is no accident that the most wondrously powerful *murtis*, particularly in the form of sculptures, are not just 'objects' of reverence, worship or even meditation but show the very gods they represent *in states of meditation*. A *murti* of this sort is not just a particular divinity given a characteristic human form that enables one to recognise, name and worship it as this or that 'god'. Instead its form is spiritually crafted to reveal the nature taken by the human form when it itself becomes an *embodiment* of particular states and qualities of meditative union with God – with the divine as such. Murti meditation is not 'worship' understood as mere 'obeisance' to a particular divinity through its image. Nor is it even meditation 'of' the divine in the form of a particular divinity. It is co-resonance with a divinity – one whose image is crafted in such a way that its whole bodily form and bearing itself embodies a profound resonance with the divine as such. Sivananda again:

"Even as you can catch the sound waves of people all over the world through the radio receiving set, it is possible to commune with the all-pervading Lord through the medium of an idol. The divinity of the all-pervading God is vibrant in every atom of creation. There is not a speck of space where he is not."

Just as a radio is more than a box of electronic parts but a vehicle of transmission, so is a Murti. And just as the images on a television screen are not inside the 'box' itself but relayed to it from without, so is the Murti itself an embodied transmission of spiritual truth carried on the waves of the divine-cosmic aether. Meditation of its bodily form (Rupa) is a way of entering into resonance with it, a resonance that can be tuned to different frequencies and 'channels', and that result in feeling experiences, visions and 'hearings'. It was such hearings ('Shruti'), borne of meditative inner silence, that first inspired the *words* of the Vedas, and all the world's holy scriptures.

To those capable of entering into deep inner silence and resonance with the *murti* – on any number of different wavelengths of spiritual attunement - its visible form will transform before their eyes. It will cease to be a mere object of their worshipful gaze, but communicate wordless wisdom to them through its own gaze. Indeed it will also speak to them directly – in the form of 'hearings' transmitted to their inner ear. To come to know the divine through meditating the *murti* of a chosen divinity is a truly profound and ever-new experience – an inexhaustible source of revelations, and not the mere repetition of a prescribed ritual. The *murti* itself ceases to be a mere image or 'idol' of a divinity. Instead through it, the divinity itself becomes one's most intimate partner and most revered Guru in meditating, understanding and experiencing the divine – capable of answering one's deepest personal or religious questions through the knowing awareness it embodies and transmits, both in inner silence and through the word, inwardly heard. 'Puja' – ritual worship – is unthinkable without 'idol worship' – sitting in the presence of the *murti* and using one's whole body and all its senses to resonate with the awareness it embodies and transmits.

Through *co-resonance*, 'idol worship' becomes an experience of the particular truth of Tantric Puja – that 'to worship a god is to become that god'.

"Regular worship, Puja and other modes of demonstrating our inner feeling recognition of Divinity in the idol unveils the Divinity latent in it. This is truly a wonder and a miracle. The idol speaks. It will answer your questions and solve your problems. The God in you has the power to awaken the latent Divinity in the idol ... Puja makes the idol shine with Divine resplendence. God is then enshrined in the idol ... the idol will perform miracles. The place where it is installed is at once transformed into a temple."

Sivananda

As Sivananda also reminds us, a Sanskrit word for meditative contemplation is 'Upasana' – which simply means 'sitting near'. The meaning and value of Murti meditation in ritual worship or Puja derives from the basic act of 'sitting near' the Murti of a god or divinity – for doing so brings us into the nearness and presence of God and Divinity.

"Upasana is approaching the chosen ideal or object of worship by meditating on it in accordance with the teachings (Shastras) and the Guru ... Upasana helps the devotee to sit near the Lord or to commune with him. It purifies the heart and steadies the mind. It fills the mind with ... pure love for the Lord. It gradually transmutes man into a divine being."

Yet for those to whom 'meditation' is merely a method of steadying the mind and calming the soul, and not also a matter of feeling the Divine from the very *heart* of one's soul – a medium of *living relationship* uniting the Self with a divine Other – such spiritual words will mean nothing without Upasana – sitting in the nearness of a material Murti, and experiencing it in all its wonders. For the sitter or Upasaka, after the ritual process of lighting oil lamps and scenting the air with incense, the meditational process begins with ensouling their own body and breathing with ever-greater awareness, particularly of those regions of their body that feel tired or tense, muddied or dissonant in tone. The sitter then ensouls the body of the Murti with their own awareness, using their own body to outwardly sense and resonate with it from without and within. In time the Murti will in turn ensoul the inwardness of the sitter's body from within and from without - allowing them to feel their own fleshly form as no less a manifestation of the divine-cosmic aether around them than the material form of the Murti itself. Union with the divinity ensouling the Murti comes to a climax when the worshipper kneels to touch the foot of the Murti, and peers up at its face allowing an even more powerful direct transmission of awareness from it – one that will pervade if not overwhelm the body and mind of the worshipper, bringing with it not only a culmination and ultimate consecration of the union they have experienced through the sitting, but an experiential answer to the deepest questions they may have felt or consciously meditated in the course of it. "The basic movement of the life of dialogue is the turning towards the other." (Martin Buber).

'Worship' is a turning to the Other – whether the face of a human other or the divine other – from our innermost Self. Indeed the very word 'worship' derives from the Indo-European root *wer* or *uer* – 'to turn'. The turning point in 'idol worship' comes when the worshipper first turns to outwardly face and/or inwardly sense the Murti, in turn to be turned – transformed – by it. In essence *there is no such thing* as 'idol worship' – only a turning to the divinity ensouling the idol, allowing us in turn to be ensouled with and by that divinity.

Notes:

* An advertisement (2007) showing a dark-skinned neo-Mayan tribe worshipping the image of a leading branded ice-cream bar and ending with the slogan 'I am a worshipper'.

References:
Swami Sivananda *The Philosophy and Significance of Idol Worship* Divine Life Society 1960

EXPERIENCES OF HINDU WORSHIP
from *The Awakening of a Devi* by Silya Muischneek

The strength and power reaching me through the *murti* of Mahakali is so profound that each day I feel her resonance empowering me more, staying a little longer within my beingness, moulding, forming, enlightening my being. So deeply differently an enlivening presents itself with each new meditation. I earnestly and longingly await those chosen times where I can allow myself to sit every morning, and especially at night, in and at my soul-shrine, my heart-temple. To be able to enter those deeply intimate, clarifying, most special soul-meetings are my life's true glorifications, its ever ongoing celebrations. They lead me to ever new spaces, reaching new actualities within the manifestation-potential of Shiva-Shakti. After each sitting meditation I arrive at a deeper resonance, which carries and stays with me ever further into daily life, subtly vibrating within and around me - keeping me in safety.

Beloved Shiva calls me deep within, leading me to kiss the ever deeper space, falling down within, in broadening and widening solitude, all safe and basic solid. Shiva murti meditation touches my silent source inwardly. I bow and listen all quietly – repeating *Om Namah Shivaya* – and let myself be guided through yet-unknown huge and darker 'inner' spaces, in which I feel led down, deep deep within. Mahakali, while I sing her mantra, brings me to smile ever so broadly, straightening my inner posture and bringing a most clear, vital and shining light. She is the awakener and the assurance of my beingness, confidently she embodies all of my individuality. Shiva on the other hand, is the awareness beholder of my whole existence – touching and being my deepest source. What I experience as his majestic earnestness, most tender and serenely vibrating facial expression – not yet smiling – floods out of his awareness-presence to offer me the most silent lasting peace. I drink within this silence an ever a-newing power, where he beholds each atom at its space-time-spot, eliciting new sounds of silence within this space and time, and with them new colours of light, all womb-like and hidden.

The transformations on Shiva's face photographed by Acharya during puja are more than remarkable, truly amazingly powerful and telling. It shows that there is not the slightest separation, no gap to be bridged between awareness and all that is manifestly forming as the touchable and visible – which is an expressiveness of the inner sound and inner silence where light and breath meet within this actualising world, creating it every second anew, afresh and different.

After midnight, very late last night while sitting down at the shrine, it was within the very first moment – looking at my new Shiva murti from India - that all around and within this murti started to glow – incredibly vivid, all translucent and extremely fluid, thus coming to ever more radiant shining. I felt tears coming into my eyes, to finally be entering the aliveness of this new Shiva murti and the throbbing I felt on my forehead in the very first days knowing Acharya came back. While meditating, Shiva's face shifted through many very different facial-expressions, rapidly and extremely fast, while kind of a air-like, goldish-white translucent 'fabric', moving vibrating like a wind, covered Shiva's beautified, fully alive, deeply bliss-filled face. This wind-like light 'fabric' all freshly, draw over his face ever new changing, transforming into ever more shining. Some actualisations, aspects – where perceived as being purely feminine in their kind, starting to teach me directly. Shiva's manifestation-expressions smiled softly and smiled serenity, so richly auspicious, then again infecting me to instantly laugh inside – leaving me all astonished. I wondered if within all these so clearly differing, individualised expressions, I might recognise my 'own' known face too, which I did not.

For the first time, after meditating my Shiva murti last night, I touched Shiva's right hand, which rests on his knee. Acharya told me that he touches Shiva's foot for some time after ending his meditative *puja* and that it is then that he receives, perceives and conceives the most intense, intimate, glorious and immediately life-relevant teachings. Thinking of this, my right hand touched Shiva's hand after my meditation. What I felt then was the most wonderful power overcoming me. Shiva's face grew more and more vibrating. Where was He? Where was I? Where this I and where this Shiva? All within one space, one room, one heart, one soul, one time, though still so different. The Shiva *murti* broadened, brightened and became so much more vitally alive in an almost fleshly sense, though all as pure light and in a purely androgynous form. Such wonders of vital, new and extraordinary experiencing are touching my inner heart ever more and I feel my eyes opening up, widening and broadening from within.

My posture becomes straighter and upright, straightening from within. And while reading Acharya's textbooks I see ever and again a golden light overflowing the pages, covering the words, and my hands and fingers engage in different mudras, guiding me to enter a deeper, more comprehensive awareness. I am completely flooded by this wonder of Shiva's grace.

Today while doing extended Shiv puja and murti darshan, my soul-body grew larger, broader and very much lighter – losing the stamp of physical age. I felt myself growing stronger – from within *and* without, reaching and extending with a not only far more up-right posture, but also felt as if this expansion knows no bodily boundaries this body in this space-time.

This body seemed to beyond-itself, each cell a whirling breathing, like an ever new little universe of its own – expanding.

Feeling myself as space itself, sides and directions of space were all one – there was 'as much' of a 'in-front' space as was there was behind, no less a down than an up. I could say it was all-round circling space – therefore free of sides – but for me it seemed there as this space had no 'form' any more at all – not even a circling form. I see it is hard for me to find the right words – but I was also seeing *this ongoing forming* of things as signs or *linga* in the way you refer to – when a chair is not chair – but more like a continuous chair-ing?! No fixed forms to see as such, neither as space, nor as 'objects' in it.

In this way I came to see Shiva's murti too, lose its material density and melt into one form-ing along with the room, with me, with the wall – with no more objects simply standing around besides or separate from each other – but with their differencing nature continuing to presence. All felt as if it were floating as and within a warm subtly whitish light – in which differing colours softened their boundaries of red and blue and became like *one* 'melody' of colour, yellow and green being *one* 'tone' – and no more colours separate. This space and everything in it as a wave – breathing-rainbowed light.

In this awareness I was reminded of a symbol which I saw painted in front of several house entrances during my travels in India – the sign of the atom. I can't say why exactly this symbol comes to my mind, seeing space loosing its commonly perceived character of being filled with objects. Maybe it is because my feeling of this constantly new forming of objects, from a freer space – a very profound 'beginning' - the point where matter first comes to light as we see it? The con-firmation dance of atoms – in the whirling light of awareness itself.

While being aware of this 'one-ing' of space with its emerging matter, I also felt a deeper more secure emotion of being at home within this body – thus capable of a truer belongingness to all there is. Still feeling like a visiting 'client' in the root meaning one who is 'called' – called to this earthly plane. Yet I felt as 'at home' 'here' as also 'there' in that other plane. Is this not the real meaning of 'coming home'?

THE MEDITATIVE LIFE OF THE TRUE HINDU

The meditative life is one in which at all times we identify with the very essence of the Divine – which is nothing but Awareness as such.

That means learning to distinguish awareness as such from each and every thing we are aware of.

To do this we need only remember that our awareness of any thing or thought, sensation or perception, feeling or emotion, *is not itself* a thing or thought, *not itself* a sensation or perception, not itself an image or emotion. Awareness as such is *innately free* of all the things and thoughts, sensations and perceptions, images and emotions we happen to be aware 'of'.

The name 'Shiva' points to the truth that awareness is what 'lies behind' (SHI) all things and can therefore free us from or 'cut asunder' (SHVI) our attachment to any thing we are aware of.

That is why Shiva, as the light of pure awareness, is associated in the Tantric tradition with absolute Freedom.

Awareness transcends all that we are aware of. Only through identification with this 'transcendent' nature of awareness [Shiva] can we also take full delight in every thing and being that we are aware of – knowing it as a mirror and manifestation of the Divine Awareness, a unique shape and a unique face of that Awareness.

Only then can we experience the Divine Awareness as not only 'transcendent' (transcending each and every thing we are aware of) but also 'immanent' (present within each and every thing).

The name 'Shiva' does not denote a divine being or god 'with' awareness. For God as Shiva IS awareness – that Divine Awareness which is the source of all beings.

What the name Shiva does denote is a fundamental aspect of the Divine Awareness – its own self-recognition or 'I'-ness. For knowing itself in and as all things and beings, it is their very Self. And knowing our innermost Self or 'I' as identical with the Divine 'I' is the experience of 'Shiv-a-wareness'.

If meditation means identifying with the Divine Awareness that IS God, then the worshipful life consists in recognising that Awareness as our innermost Self or 'I', and in recognising that 'I' as identical with the 'I'-ness of the Divine – with Shiva.

In pursuing this aim, the traditional Hindu practice of *puja* (worship) in the form of *murti* meditation is a most important and powerful means – making possible at any time a direct experience of the divine as pure awareness.

THE TENETS OF TANTRIC HINDUISM

Hindu Tantric theology, and in particular the schools of Tantric Hinduism derived from Kashmir and known collectively as 'Kashmir Shaivism', understand the essential nature of the Divine as **Pure Awareness** (personified by the god *Shiva*) and its **Pure Power** (the goddess or *Shakti*).

"THE BEING OF ALL THINGS RECOGNISED IN AWARENESS IN TURN DEPENDS ON AWARENESS."

Abhinavagupta

GOD IS NOT A SUPREME BEING 'WITH' AWARENESS. GOD *IS* AWARENESS.

JUST AS THERE CAN BE NOTHING 'OUTSIDE' SPACE SO THERE CAN BE NOTHING OUTSIDE AWARENESS, NOTHING OUTSIDE GOD.

JUST AS EVERYTHING EXISTS WITHIN AWARENESS, SO DOES EVERYTHING EXIST WITHIN GOD.

JUST AS AWARENESS IS WITHIN EVERYTHING, SO GOD IS WITHIN EVERYTHING.

THE OCEAN OF AWARENESS

Just as an ocean is the source of all the fish and other life forms within it, so is the Awareness that IS 'God' the source of all beings within it. All beings dwell *within* this Divine Awareness as all fish dwell within the ocean. And just as fish are formed from the very stuff of the ocean, so are all beings formed from the divine God-stuff of awareness. All the fish and life forms within the ocean are connected to one another through it, not just because they all dwell within it, but because they are all self-expressions of it. Similarly, all beings are connected to one another both outwardly and inwardly. They are connected outwardly because they all dwell within the Divine Awareness, and connected inwardly because the essential Self of each being is its nature as a Self-expression of the same Divine Awareness. Yet if God is the Divine Awareness, and this Awareness is compared in this way to an ocean, then it makes no more sense to think of God as a single *being*, than it does to think of the ocean as a single supreme *fish*.

THE CO-CREATION OF GOD AND MAN

"The long road to finding God. Somewhere along the line, they [human beings] achieve Freedom by identifying with Shiva. The circle is complete – as once Shiva identified with them to give them freedom. As his selves or creations come to self awareness as him, he comes to self awareness as his selves."

Andrew Gara

In the beginning was that God who knows no beginning or end. That God which is not 'nothing' but is also no 'thing' and no 'being', for it is the source of ALL beings. This God is not a being 'with' awareness. This God IS awareness as such – infinite and unbounded.

This unbounded awareness alone is the ultimate and unsurpassable reality (Anuttara), for it is the very condition for our awareness of any specific thing or being, world or universe whatsoever – including our very awareness of ourselves, our bodies and mind, feelings and thoughts. This Awareness alone is therefore also the very essence of The Divine – of 'God'.

Yet within the womb of this Divine Awareness – the true meaning of 'Shiva' as the Great God or Mahadeva – infinite creative potentialities lie darkly hidden – this womb of potentiality or power being the great mother goddess or Mahadevi that is known as 'Kali'.

At first dimly sensed within the light of the Divine Awareness that is Shiva, these potentialities gradually took the form of ever clearer, more lucid and light-filled dreams – dreams of infinite potential worlds, infinite potential realities and infinite potential beings – individual consciousnesses or 'Jiva'.

Shiva not only embraced all these potential worlds and beings in the transcendent light of his unbounded awareness – but through that light automatically released them from the womb of the Great Goddess into free and autonomous self-actualisation, as Her autonomous powers of action or 'Shaktis'.

The countless individualised selves or Jiva that make up our physical world of human beings then evolved through a long road – one which led them to falsely believe that they were entities separate and apart from one another and from the Divine, beings whose womb or matrix was Matter or Energy and not The Mother and her power of potentiality.

The Jiva even came to believe that their physical actuality was the product of some cosmic accident and that even consciousness was their personal private property – not a uniquely individualised portion of the Divine Awareness that is Shiva.

Hypnotised by letting their awareness become focused and concentrated on their outer, physical reality, they gradually lost any sense of other planes or dimensions of reality and their awareness became restricted to their physical minds and bodies.

However, they also secretly yearned to feel again their connection with the darkness of the Divine Mother from whose womb they emerged, with the light of Divine Awareness that had released them from it, and with all those countless other planes and dimensions of awareness that the Great Mother Goddess and the Great God – Mahadevi and Mahadeva – had jointly given birth to.

So began the long search among human beings to re-find 'God'. Along this way, great teachers showed them the way, teaching them through the wisdom of Yoga, Mantra and Tantra to identify with the pure Awareness that is the Divine – knowing that by doing so they would totally free their awareness from identification with their limited physical consciousness and all its contents.

The Divine, aware of this in advance, had already prepared the way by dreaming itself in the human form of Shiva. Yet as once that Divine Awareness had dreamt itself not just in the form of Shiva but that of each embodied human soul or Jiva, so now human beings began to dream of their own divine source, yearning to once again feel themselves and each other as a part of the Divine Awareness and not as separate and apart from it and each other.

As once the Divine Awareness had creatively dreamed them, so now they began to creatively dream its manifold forms, letting them freely emerge into the light from within the dark depths of their own maternal souls. Thus humankind gave birth to the gods as the gods had once given birth to them. Some of these gods represented the many faces, bodies and qualities of the Divine Awareness as such. Others represented only the limiting ego-awareness of human beings, their experience of themselves as souls bound to and bounded by their own bodies. For releasing them into freedom, Shiva had also allowed each individualised soul or Jiva to freely fall into the bondage of contracted awareness, forgetting its own source in the Divine. As a result, the Jivas found themselves needing to seek and re-find 'God' – the freedom of that unbounded, pure and Divine Awareness which transcends body and mind, transcends all limited identities and contents of consciousness.

God as Shiva is the Divine Light of a pure awareness that is inseparable from and yet quite distinct from all there is to be conscious or aware OF – and can therefore simply De-Light in it.

Yet if the Divine experiences itself as a self or Jiva who has come to experience their self AS that very Awareness – as Shiva – the circle is completed. The delight of both Shiva and Jiva are conjoined as the absolute freedom

(Moksha) and pure bliss (Ananda) of the Divine Awareness. *Both* now experience themselves as an Awareness that is neither 'dual' nor 'non-dual', neither separate nor indistinctly merged, but both distinct and inseparable – like two sides of a coin, or like two lovers in a permanent and unbreakable embrace.

Judaism, Christianity and Islam – are theistic and dualistic, asserting that God is a supreme creator being separate from 'His' creations. Buddhism is a-theistic and non-dualistic, denying the reality of a Supreme Being. It is also nihilistic in the essential sense – negating the existence of any fixed identities in the form of things, selves or beings and asserting that the highest truth is Emptiness or Non-Being understood as 'No-thing-ness'. Tantric theology understands the Divine neither as Being nor Non-Being; neither as a single Supreme Being nor as a multiplicity of beings but as that Absolute Awareness that is the source of all things and all beings. That Awareness is Absolute because it embraces not only all that is actual – all that has Being – but the reality of all that is potential. For 'Non-Being' is not simply 'Emptiness', 'Formlessness' – 'No-thing-ness' – but a womb of inexhaustible potentiality – the divine 'Mother' of all actual existing things. It is the Light of Awareness that releases these potentialities into their own free and autonomous actualisation and Being.

RELIGION AS UNIFIED FIELD AWARENESS

Awareness is not something that dwells 'in' us, bounded by our bodies. We ourselves dwell *in* awareness in the same way that objects exist in space. Both the physical space we sense around our bodies and the psychic spaces we sense within them are subjective spaces – the spaces of awareness within which we are aware of things and without which we could be aware of nothing. We exist in awareness – inner and outer – in the same way that the elements of our outer and inner world can only be experienced in spaces – inner and outer. All space being subjective, there is essentially only one space from which we emerge and in which we exist, an unbounded space of divine awareness. Christianity understood this 'Awareness Principle' through the metaphor of 'The Kingdom' that is both outside us and inside us. Buddhism understood it through the principle that form and the formlessness of space are inseparable. Kashmir Shaivism understood it through the principle of *Shiva-Shakti*. *Shiva* – the unbounded, bodiless space of divine awareness (*akula*) in which every body exists, and which embraces the totality (*kula*) of bodies that make up the "embodied cosmos" (Muller-Ortega) or *Shakti* of *Shiva*.

All awareness is awareness of things sensuous, bodily. Even the most abstract of thoughts has its own 'body' – its own sensuous shape and form. But the awareness of things bodily, including our own bodies, is not itself anything bodily, but is something essentially bodiless – like the formlessness of space. How then do bodily things form themselves in the first place? Because formless awareness that we perceive as empty space is not in fact empty but is a fullness of formative potentials. Such potentials – all potentials – only exist in awareness, and do so as potential shapes and forms of awareness. Formless awareness gives birth to form from these potentials. As the formlessness of space it shapes itself into bodily forms. *Shakti* is the very power and process of actualisation of these potentials – the bodiless, formless awareness of *Shiva* giving form to itself into countless bodily shapes. We are such bodily shapes of awareness. As such we are not only formed from divine awareness space. We exist in that space as we exist in space itself. And that space exists within us just as we exist within it. We are each a unified space or field of awareness, our bodies a mere boundary between the awareness we exist within and the awareness that exists within us. To perceive an object with awareness is to perceive it in its place – in the surrounding space in which alone it stands out or 'exists'. But look around at people – people you know and people on the street – and you will see something different. You will see from their bodies – indeed from the very look on their face – that they do not sense themselves as existing *in* awareness, just as they do in space. They feel their awareness as something that exists only within their body's fleshly boundaries – where even there it may be contracted to the narrowest of spaces in their heads. Spiritual 'enlightenment' is nothing but the decontraction of the sensed awareness space in which we exist and which exists within us – its outer expansion and inward expansion or 'inpansion'. The bounded inner space of awareness was named by the Greek word *psyche*, the Latin *anima*, and the Sanskrit *jiva*. The outer space by the Greek word *pneuma*, the Latin *spiritu*s, and the Sanskrit *akasha*.

Every religion has its sacred places and spaces. Buildings are erected in such places to mark out and bound the sacred spaces within them. The word 'temple' (Latin *templum*) means such a consecrated inner space. A building such as a temple is also a shaping of space, one which lends a specific quality both to the space within it and to the space of the landscape or cityscape in which it is set. The dome of St. Peter lends a different quality to the spaces within and around it to that of a Gothic cathedral, a Buddhist stupa or a Hindu temple. The same principle applies to the objects set within such holy spaces. They also, like the objects in our own homes, lend a specific quality to the space in which they are set and have their place. Is there anything at all that can truly unite all religions, given the quite different quality of the awareness spaces they shape in such specific ways – through their languages and images, rituals and sacred places? The only thing that could unite them in essence would be a *unified field theology* of awareness – one which recognises the embrace of divine awareness in space as such. The essential religious philosophy or 'theosophy' of what I call The New Yoga, like that of 'Kashmir Shaivism', is such a unified field theology – comprehending the unity of outer and inner awareness space, of 'The Kingdom' outside and inside, of *pneuma* and *psyche*, of formlessness and form, of potentiality (*dynamis*) and its actualisation (*energeia*), of a*kula* and *kula*, of *Shiva* and *Shakti*. Unified field theology, by virtue of offering a unified field theory of awareness and its expression as energy and matter, also unifies spirituality and science, psychology and physics. But being a unified field theory of awareness the heart of such a unified field theology must be *unified field awareness* as such. Through The New Yoga each individual can come to experience themselves as existing within divine awareness as within space. Similarly, they can come to experience that divine awareness within them – as their body's very inwardness of soul. By uniting the spatial fields of their awareness with one another, they can not only realise a state of decontracted and divine awareness for themselves – they can also unite their own fields of awareness with those of others. Conversely, it is by cultivating and experiencing field-resonance with the awareness of others that they can truly realise themselves – living in and out of unified field awareness that unites them with one another, inwardly and outwardly. Hence the New Yogic practice of pair meditation as field-resonation with the awareness of others. For it is above all "Where two or more are gathered in My Name" that the unified field awareness that is the very essence of divinity – under whatever name – can be most deeply felt, most broadly expanded and most powerfully embodied. A unified world religion cannot be achieved through ecumenical dialogues or doctrinal disputes, nor can it take the form of some eclectic or 'syncretic' religion. Neither theological liberalism and heterodoxy nor conservative orthodoxy and 'inquisitions' bear any relation to the type of genuine meditative inquiry required to research, rethink and refind the common source and essence of religious practices and symbols – in all their different historical and cultural forms. This common source and essence can only be found in the direct experience of unified field awareness. What the world requires now is a new world religion of the sort hoped for by Hermann Hesse, one based on a newly thought theology. This can only be a *unified field theology* which, whatever its historic roots, is based on a renewed experience of the divine as the *foundational* and *unified field awareness* in which all worlds arise and all beings dwell – as it dwells within them. The true body of the human being is a *unified field body* of awareness uniting three fields of awareness – a *field of exteriority* manifest as our awareness of the physical space around us, a field of interiority which we feel as the spacious inwardness of our own soul – and the field of *unbounded interiority* into which our own inwardness of soul leads. This field of unbounded interiority is also the all-surrounding field that constitutes the *soul world* as such – that which lies behind all that we perceive in the exterior space around us. It is within this field of unbounded and all-surrounding 'interiority' that all seemingly 'exterior' spaces of awareness – all space-time worlds – first open up. Our unified field body is the singular field-boundary of awareness uniting all three fields. Yet precisely *as* this very boundary it is itself essentially boundless – a *unified field awareness*.

THE HISTORICAL EVOLUTION
OF HUMAN AWARENESS

If you turn a corner at a crossroads, the road you see ahead of you is now different from what you beheld before you took the turning. And were you to stop and look back, the road behind you would not be the same road you had been travelling before turning the corner. Imagine however that you had forgotten the turn you had taken, and believed firmly that the road behind and ahead of you had always been exactly as you saw them right now – from your current perspective and in terms of the current direction or 'road' being taken by your awareness. This is exactly the way humanity views its past and future 'history' – from the current nature of human awareness and the current road it is taking – quite unaware of previous turning points in the evolutionary road of that awareness.

The most crucial such turning point was the evolution of ego-awareness – which is why we falsely imagine all past human beings to have perceived the world in the same ego-centred way that we do today, and why today's scientists, scholars and philosophers can no longer understand ancient religions and philosophies that arose from a completely different type of awareness. In the forgotten 'pre-history' of human awareness – long before the development of ego-awareness – human beings had a completely different awareness of space, time and of history itself. They dwelled in a much broader 'time-space' of awareness than we do – one in which 'dead' ancestors, for example, were experienced as being as alive as ever, and in which a living memory was maintained of the emergence of the Earth itself out of the divine awareness itself – in particular through the higher awareness of 'gods' whose reality was still experienced directly by human beings, not just in their inner life but in their outer world itself. Cosmic bodies such as Sun, Moon were not just interpreted intellectually as symbols of conscious divinities but immediately felt and sensed *as* shining divinities (the very words *divinity*, *deva* and *devi* having their root in the Sanskrit word for 'shining'). What we take as a purely 'outer' world of objects in space-time was experienced much as we now experience the 'inner world' of our dreams – for it had not yet taken on the same degree of 'objective' fixity as our current waking reality. Instead, that outer world retained a subjective, ever-shifting or dreamlike character, one not yet experienced as separate from the dreams and 'inner' life of human beings.

Human beings can fly in dreams but they cannot actually capture, kill or eat dream pigs, let alone flying ones. The development of 'ego-awareness' came about because of what it essentially was – a new capacity of human beings to *contract* the fluid, dreamlike character of the time-space in which they dwelled, one that enabled them to precisely focus or target their awareness 'in' time and in space. Only those who could do so could truly 'hit' their target with their spears, bows and arrows. As they learned to do so, it was not only human beings who changed, but the world too and the other creatures within it. Like human beings, the predecessors of our pigs formed physical bodies from their dream bodies or soul bodies. These were bodies that could be and were 'killed' by other creatures and by human beings, albeit with the full awareness that no being can ever be killed, for its 'spirit' survives, and does so with its own dream body or soul body fully intact.

This turning point in the evolution of human awareness had already been reached by what we see today as early or 'prehistoric' man. What is not recognised is that the earliest civilisations called upon higher powers and the powers of their own awareness to imbue matter itself with greater solidity and durability. Their ruler priests however, necessarily formed a separate 'caste' of their own, distinct from hunters, farmers or warriors, for it was their task to forge religious and artistic cultures that still preserved a deeper, spiritual awareness of time, the gods and creation of a sort that preceded ego-awareness. From it they also seeded sciences and technologies that drew directly from this older awareness. Some of these ruler-priests were indeed 'gods' incarnate – higher consciousnesses from other planes, planets and dimensions of reality, disguised in human form. Without their knowledge, humanity would have made no agricultural, cultural, intellectual or technical progress and some of the earliest known civilisations – for example that of Mesopotamia and the Indus Valley, would not have existed.

The early ruler priests who came to Earth from other planets and planes of awareness required well-trained warriors and whole armies with which to defend themselves and their peoples, their cultures and civilisations, against others types of ruler – rulers in whom ego-awareness had taken hold at the expense of higher spiritual awareness – and for whom priests served merely as advisers, soothsayers and sources of useful spiritual and technical 'know-how'. Thus came about an era of great battles for the soul of humanity, recorded in many ancient 'mythological' dramas. Having the technical products of their own knowledge turned against them, the power of the ruler priests waned. Yet the priesthoods themselves preserved their knowledge to different degrees, and ensured that contact with higher realities and consciousnesses could be maintained. No longer incarnate in the flesh, the gods became incarnate, when called for, in stone idols – able to communicate with the priests through them. Thus did the so-called 'idol worship' begin. Only later were stone sculptures of the sort well-known in ancient Egypt regarded as mere lifeless images or iconic representations of the gods. By far the most important turning point in the evolution of human awareness came when the human ego began to experience itself as a self or 'I' totally independent of its own source in higher beings and in a larger, divine-spiritual awareness. Thus it was that the ego itself came to be worshipped as a god in its own right – or rather to submit itself to a deified paternal 'super ego' wielding judgemental power over the ego itself, and ruling men and all other creatures of the Earth in the way a king ruled others. This God was seen as having created all beings and 'made' the world in the way a man might make a bow and arrow, through the active application of focussed ego-awareness. Since the ego experiences itself as 'owning' its own awareness and as the independent agent of its actions, understanding was lost of the natural way in which all creative activity, including ego-activity, is something that emerges within the womb of a pre-egoic awareness, one that is not the *private property* of any agent, ego or God.

The deification of ego-awareness was heralded historically by the transformation of the Hebrew god *Jahweh*, hitherto both a tribal god and one of the group of gods known as the *Elohim*, into a monotheistic Father God and a pure abstraction of egohood or 'I'-ness. Only much later did Karl Marx understand the whole development of ego awareness as one which ran parallel with the transition from "primitive communism" – harmonious property-sharing tribal communities – to a sequence of social and economic orders all based on different forms of private property ownership, whether in the form of slave societies, feudalism or capitalism. Right from the beginning, this led to competition for land, resources and human labour itself. The Jewish god-image served first of all to reflect the jealous, competitive, aggressive and unpredictable characteristics of the infantile human ego. Later, 'God' became a controlling 'Father' or superego, using religious regulations to reign in the otherwise rampant and still infantile human ego itself. The Jewish prophets foresaw the need for humanity to develop ego-awareness, but also anticipated that it would need balancing. Christianity was called for in order to balance the judgemental and punitive character of the Father God with characteristics of love and compassion. In India, however, developments took a quite different course. The 'Rishis' – 'seer-hearers' and priest-kings of ancient Indian civilisation – had preserved an inherited pre-egoic awareness and knowledge and passed it on to other cultures. Instead of identifying God with a 'Father' on high and his one Son, the Divine was identified with the source and innermost Self of every human being. Religion then, established its deeper purpose of re-linking human ego-awareness with its source in the inner self and the Divine Awareness. Much later, when a militant Christianity ruled Europe through the power of Rome, its military expansion was halted by the still 'heathen' Teutonic tribes – enabling Germany to serve as the European centre of an artistic and philosophical culture that retained the inherited knowledge or 'Gnosis' of earlier pre-Roman

Christianity and the pre-Judaic religious traditions of the East.

The *Shiva Sutras* are the foundational scripture of the Hindu Tantric tradition of 'Kashmir Shaivism'. The first aphoristic 'thread' or 'Sutra' that appears in them is a single, finite word in Sanskrit. Yet this is a word that makes an extraordinary statement – an 'infinite statement'. The word is 'Chaitanyamatma'. What this one word says is that the awareness of an aware being ('Chetana') is itself the essential 'nature', 'is-ness' or 'self' ('Atman') of that being – the ultimate reality behind the word 'I'. 'Chaitanyamatma' can be translated both as a statement ('Awareness is the Self') or simply as a compound noun – 'Awareness Self'. Either way, the message is the same. This is that 'Being a Self' means not only 'Being Aware' but 'Being Awareness' – identifying with Awareness as one's very Self or 'I'. The self as 'ego' takes the dual form of a subjectively experienced 'self' and/or an objectified self – its account of itself as part of its experienced world. The Awareness Self, on the other hand is ultimately identical with Shiva – that ultimate or divine awareness that embraces all selves, including the limited ego, all things and all worlds. Both as subject and as object of awareness the egoic 'I' has its source within that Self which does not 'have' awareness but *is* awareness – a universal field of awareness. The little word "I" can thus not only give expression to the individual as an isolated ego but as a singular centre of this field – a "singularity of awareness" which expresses its entirety.

HINDUISM, GLOBALISATION AND 'YOGA'

What passes as 'Yoga' today has become little more than a global commercial industry – a respectable bourgeois 'opium' for the middle classes of East and West. The New Yoga of Awareness is no part of this global industry. Instead it aims at subverting and overturning the entire framework of global capitalism itself – through a global revolution in awareness. To achieve this the very concept of 'yoga' itself must be renewed and become something 'global' in a very different way – not as a worldwide industry exploiting one or more Asian spiritual traditions but as an entirely new global world outlook and way of thinking – one that gives new expression to the ancient wisdom traditions of all races, religions, cultures and continents – Eastern and Western, Northern and Southern, Aryan and Semitic.

In the revolutionary social, cultural and political movements of the 1960's and 70's the word 'awareness' was associated with 'raising' people's 'awareness' or 'consciousness' of uncomfortable political and economic facts and events – thereby confronting them with the need for worldwide revolution. In what I term 'The New Yoga' or 'New Millennium Yoga' the political importance attached to the term 'awareness' does not simply lie in 'awareness raising' of this sort – raising awareness *of* something. Instead it refers to the raising of a new global awareness, one that has to do with the transcendental and liberatory nature of awareness *as such* rather than anything we are aware of. Therein lies its link with the Tantric 'Gnosis' or inner wisdom tradition, this being the sole tradition which recognised that awareness is the ultimate reality behind all things, and that only through awareness as such – 'pure' or 'transcendental' awareness – can the individual liberate their consciousness from bondage to any particular thing or things that they experience or are aware *of.* The New Yoga recognises that this type of 'transcendental' awareness is not just a means of individual liberation, salvation or 'enlightenment' however, but the only way to 'save the world' from the ravages of global capitalism. The New Yoga of Awareness is therefore not just a 'revolutionary' new interpretation of the yogic tradition known as 'Tantra'. It is a *Revolutionary Yoga* – aimed at peacefully promoting global revolution – saving the world – through the dawning of a New Awareness.

A GLOBAL REVOLUTION IN AWARENESS

Revolution means 'turning round'. Only through this New Awareness can the topsy-turvy world of global capitalism be turned around – a world in which science has literally turned reality 'on its head' by treating awareness itself as a by-product of the head and brain, a world in which ever more costly medical drugs and technologies are responsible for ever more deaths, totally ignoring the relation between health and awareness; a world in which 'psychology' no longer even recognises the reality of the soul or 'psyche'. It is also a world in which ever-more advanced and easily available technologies of communication go hand in hand with a dearth – indeed the near-death – of spiritual culture – and in which education systems generate ever-greater historical, cultural, and spiritual ignorance, not to mention linguistic illiteracy. The New Yoga is revolutionary because, as *Education in Awareness* it is the precondition for a historical, spiritual, scientific, economic and cultural revolution – one based on an entirely new way of thinking. Meditative awareness is the sole source from which this new way of thinking can arise – a meditative thinking that is not purely calculative or technological – and that is truly rational because it does not merely serve to cynically rationalise the purposes of current political and economic interest groups. The New Yoga affirms the true and traditional aim of Yoga and Tantra as such. That aim is simply truth – personal and political, scientific and spiritual, rational and religious. That is why it goes hand in hand with what I have called 'The New Science' and 'The New Thinking' – both of which are rooted in the recognition of Awareness as the ultimate scientific and spiritual reality. The New Science and New Thinking unite Spirituality and Socialism, meditation and Marxism. Only through Marxism can we understand how the evolution and eventual domination of ego-consciousness – the idea of awareness as private property – went hand in hand with the development of class societies based on private property.

THE SUBVERSIVE NATURE OF AWARENESS

Awareness is the biggest single threat to global capitalism. For this is a system which relies for its survival on ensuring that individuals are kept so busy *doing* by selling their labour time that they have no time to become more aware – and to think more deeply – about what they are doing and why.

The result is a world in which economic wealth is paid for through time poverty, attained by economically exploiting the labour time of others, and used to pursue ever-new ways of squandering time or making more money. Consequently, people feel that they either have 'no time' or – whether super-rich or poor and unemployed – do not know what to 'do' with the time they have except squander it, reinforcing the capitalist work ethic that 'the devil makes work for idle hands'. Even most of those in 'employment' suffer from the hidden unemployment of their individual creative potentials, which can find expression only as hobbies or part-time activities. Marx is often quoted as declaring that individuals' awareness is determined by their 'social being' – their economic status in class society. For Marx this was not an eternal a-historic truth but a temporary historical truth associated with class societies. Therefore the converse truth also holds –

individuals with awareness can save the world from the stranglehold of class society in its final stage – global capitalism. For by giving themselves time to be aware they will begin to think and act in ways that can usher in what John Buchan foresaw as a "4-dimensional Communism", one that recognises that the degradation of human life begins with the exploitation or qualitative degradation of time. Only through awareness can we expand and qualitatively enrich the inner time-space of each and every moment of our lives. That is why 'meditation' – awareness time – is the frontline in the struggle for a better world, one that can come about only by empowering individuals – in whatever personal, relational, institutional, corporate or political contexts they live and work in – to resist all pressures which prevent them taking time to be aware and enriching the time they devote to themselves, their work and others.

THE SOCIAL DIMENSION
OF TANTRIC HINDUISM

Rarely do those who claim to study or practice Hindu 'tantric' teachings ever ask themselves about its social roots, and the sort of social values and awareness from which it first arose. For the universal awareness and values that are the source of any particular spiritual tradition are not identical with its symbolic forms, scriptural texts and their social and cultural context. Tantric Hinduism transcended the traditional religious culture, philosophy and social values of the 'Vedas'. That is because they were the social and cultural expression of a new universal awareness and value system – not that of the high-caste Vedic priests or 'Brahmins' but that of the Dravidian, dark-skinned, under-privileged and low-caste sections of Indian society. At the heart of this value system was the rejection of purely ritualistic forms of religion, or any form of purely hereditary or ethnic caste system, respect for women, and above all – freedom and truth. The spirituality cultivated by Hindu Tantricists, unlike those of the Vedic Brahmans and Buddhists, was based not on rejection but rather on heightened awareness of the body and its recognition and veneration as the very abode of the gods. Culturally and historically the term *tantra* initially referred to any form of treatise expressing knowledge arising directly from bodily awareness, experience and activity – whether farming, weaving, religious ritual or love-making. They reflected Marx's profound understanding of knowledge as something rooted not in material objects but in human sensuous and bodily activity. Yet through the value given in Indian culture to immediate bodily knowing were also born not only the earliest 'scientific' treatises or *tantras* relating to everyday practical skills, arts and crafts but also bodies of spiritual knowledge dealing with the highest spiritual-scientific truths and manuals of the spiritual practices or yogas needed to attain them.

A 'true teacher' or 'Satguru' was one capable of imparting such bodily knowing and its expression through the powers or 'Siddhis' it granted them. All the original, legendary 'empowered teachers' or 'Siddha-Charyas' of the Tantric tradition were not priests but low-caste farmers, artisans or labourers. Their powers were symbolised by goddesses or Shaktis (from the Sanskrit root 'Shak' – meaning capacity or power). The 'male' principle of divinity, on the other hand, was identified with pure awareness (Chit) and symbolised by the god Shiva. That is why the Tantric tradition of Kashmir Shaivism identifies the Divine Awareness neither with a male or female principle but with their dynamic and creative unity – with 'Shiva-Shakti'.

'THE NEW YOGA' AS A NEW HINDUISM

In contrast to the Torah, Bible and Koran, Hindu 'scripture' has no dogmatically restricted canon of scriptures, no supreme institution, no single spiritual founder such as an Abraham, Moses, Jesus, Buddha or Mohammed and no authoritative leader such as a Pope, Archbishop, Ayatollah or Dalai Lama. A philosophically revived and refined Tantric Hinduism can and should serve the noble and most necessary purpose of resisting 'The New Atheism' and the secular 'Monotheism of Money' that dominate today's world – along with the unquestioned assumptions of the purely technological 'science' that is its dominant 'religion'. In this way, a new Hinduism can help bring an end to the rising ocean of spiritual ignorance, and to the grave ecological devastation, economic inequalities and global mayhem that go with worship of science and technology and the monotheistic god of the Abrahamic faiths – essentially a deification of the *ego* and of the human being's narrow and limited ego-consciousness. Such a New Hinduism alone can accomplish this world-transforming aim – not through Jihad, violence or war but through the supreme principle and innate power of Awareness (Chit). 'The New Yoga of Awareness' is a new Hindu world-view which recognises that 'God' is not a supreme being 'with' awareness – a type of divine Superego. Instead God IS awareness – that pure awareness whose light is the divine Source of all beings, yet also immanent within them as their eternal and divine Self.

REVOLUTION AS 'KALI YOGA'
– THE NEW YOGA OF TIME

Time is not an 'objective' function or property of anything that is – of 'being' – but a mode of subjective awareness of what is. Yet if our lives consist of nothing but constant movement from 'one thing to another' – one activity or focus of awareness to another – then we remain fettered to ego-consciousness, with its constricted experience of time as a mere one-dimensional line in 'space-time'. This one-dimensional experience of time quite literally offers no time for a type of free and unfocussed awareness – one that could allow us to experience time itself as an expansive space of awareness – as 'time-space'. That is why 'going from one thing to another' – from one focus of awareness or action to another, is the very opposite of living a meditative life – a life of freedom and awareness. For it deprives us of what is most essential to life and time quality – namely *taking time* for *a free and unfocussed awareness* of all there is to be aware of – all there is to reflect on, look back on, look forward to and enjoy.

Today's global business culture however, is one of incessant *busyness* – a constant 'going from one thing to another'. This culture of busyness expresses the very essence of the capitalist business and economic system – which demands that people *sell* their time to an employer –

to be used at the behest of their bosses, and paid only according to its quantity and market value. In this way work becomes what Marx called 'wage slavery' – taking what is most precious to each individual – namely their time and awareness – and turning it into a mere commodity to be bought, sold, focussed and directed by the will of another. The capitalist employer seeks to extract ever more quantities of time out of their employees in order to exploit it as the source of 'surplus value' – profit – whilst at the same time demanding an ever-greater focussing or concentration of awareness on multiple tasks and objectives. The result is not just a quantitative loss of time for those things of most value to the individual, but a general diminution of time quality – and with it both quality of life and work. Along with this goes a narrowing of awareness accompanied by 'anxiety' or 'angst' (both words whose Germanic roots (*angu/angxt*) refer to 'narrowness' or *Enge* – as in the name *Eng*-land or 'narrow land').

The culture of capitalism is also one in which time is seen as something to be ever more productively *used* or *filled*. Yet the very identification of 'productivity' with speed and measurable *quantities* of times is ultimately counter-productive, diminishing *quality* of time, quality of work and quality of decision-making in all spheres of life, personal, economic and political. Actions become purely *reactive* or mere expressions of wilful or egotistic 'single-mindedness' rather than arising out of an awareness of *alternate possible actions and decisions* – the foundation of free choice and of patient and considered decisions and actions. 'Meditation' on the other hand, means *giving* ourselves time rather than *using* or *filling* time – above all giving ourselves time to come to rest in a state of *free and unfocussed awareness* – a 'pure awareness' (*chit*) unbound to any particular focus of awareness, perception or activity. In this sense, meditation is the very opposite of an *ultra-focussed* or 'single-pointed' *concentration* of awareness. Nor is meditation merely one more thing to 'make' time for in our culture of busyness. Instead, what 'meditation' means in everyday life is a strict discipline or *yoga* – the discipline of granting ourselves intervals of time between *each and every* everyday task or activity we engage in – not just as 'pauses' or 'breaks' for relaxation, entertainment or 'rest' but intervals in which we allow ourselves to *come to rest* in an expanded 'space' of free and unfocussed *awareness*. This expanded *time-space* restores our relation to time in its wholeness – *transcending* the demands and pressures dominating the present moment and encompassing both past and future as well as the immediate present – thus allowing us to reflect on and feel more deeply into all that has been, is and is yet to come.

Within the spacious expanse of a free and unfocussed awareness field we cease to be lost in any particular focus of awareness and activity, or else overburdened by a *multiplicity* of foci in the form of different life aims, daily tasks or work demands. At the same time, since this expanded time-space also encompasses and embraces *every* possible focus of our life and awareness – past, present and future – it is a source of fresh creative insights and impulses to action of a sort that do not arise from a narrow, single-pointed focus or concentration of awareness, however intense. Yet this time-space of pure, unfocussed awareness cannot be opened up in everyday life without practicing daily 'meditation' in a specific way – not just at the *beginning or end* of the day – but *between* each period of focussed awareness and activity that we engage in *during* the day.

This meditative discipline or 'yoga of time' is by nature *subversive* and *revolutionary*. It is a *Kali Yoga* (from the Sanskrit *kal* – 'time') for the *Kali Yuga* – that age which is above all characterised by a global capitalist culture designed precisely to keep people bound in a constant state of *busyness* – one in which they busily go 'from one thing to another' without ever giving themselves time to come to rest within that unbounded cosmic time-space or circumference of awareness that is the womb of the Great Mother goddess – *Ma Kali*.

BEYOND THE MONOTHEISM OF MONEY

Text of a discourse delivered
by **Acharya Peter Wilberg** to
the *Eastern Traditions Society* of
Canterbury Christ Church University
17.03.2009

The Sanskrit word *Acharya* is translated in English as 'preceptor', related to the word 'precept'. In Hinduism, an *Acharya* is a teacher or guru capable of imparting clear understandings of fundamental philosophical precepts and practices. I have been invited here today by the Eastern Traditions Society on the occasion of the Hindu festival of Holi, and in the role of *Acharya* – preceptor. I come with the aim of introducing the basic *precepts* of a radical new philosophical principle – one with *profound implications* for our understanding of life, science and religion, as well as the most *practical of applications* in fields as diverse as psychology and medicine, politics and economics, education, ecology and cosmology. I call this principle quite simply: The Awareness Principle. Evolved and refined over 35 years, it is my understanding that this new principle and its practice – what I call 'The New Yoga of Awareness' or 'New Millennium Yoga' – is capable of both renewing and integrating many different schools of Eastern thought, and in doing so, offering new answers to fundamental questions that have for long been falsely understood in the West, except amongst a few rare and great thinkers.

In Hinduism, there is no hard and fast separation between theology and philosophy, reason and revelation, spirituality and science. Hinduism is essentially 'theo-sophy' and *spiritual* science. If there is anything that might deserve the name Hindu 'fundamentalism' then, it is not a set of fanatically held beliefs, but rather an unceasing and ever-evolving quest to articulate fundamental *truth* – religious and philosophical, scientific and spiritual. The primary ethical value placed on truth affirmed already in the Rig Veda.

In this sense Hinduism, despite being regarded as one faith or world religion among others, does indeed fit the well-known motto: 'No religion higher than truth'.

In the West, truth and falsity have long been regarded as a property of propositions – of assertions, whether religious or scientific. Academics, philosophers, theologians, politicians and people of all sorts present and dispute the truth of countless propositions or assertions, beliefs and convictions. Yet they do so without beginning to question the meaning and truth of the individual words or terms employed in those propositions. Thus theists in the West debate with secularists and atheists regarding the existence or non-existence of 'God', without questioning what the word God means, even if only to them, not to mention the many different ways this word can and has been understood in cultures beyond their own. Instead there is a tacit or covert assumption that we all 'know what is meant' when the word God is used – just as we all know what we mean by the terms 'spirit' and 'soul' or even the scientific term 'energy'. This Greek-rooted term is used by New Age spiritual teachers and even scholars of Eastern thought – even physicists themselves cannot define in words what it essentially is.

In the context of the current debate about the value of religion as such, let me be clear about one fact. We do *not* live in a so-called secular society – *indeed there is no such thing* – but rather one dominated by what Marx called 'The Monotheism of Money'. Together with this goes the most irreligiously polytheistic culture humanity has ever seen. This culture is characterised by the worship of countless commodities – whether in the form of cars, pop idols and celebrity icons – or even their mere images or idols. Its polytheism has as its essence what Marx called 'the fetishism of the commodity' and with it today's culture of marketing – which turns the most basic of human values – love, freedom, soul, spirituality – into mere buzz words for advertisers. Marx also emphasised something of deep religious significance in Hinduism – which worships all things as sensory expressions of the Divine. This is the fact that we can each 'own' and enjoy things with our senses – without having to 'have' or 'own' them as private property.

Yet today even different Eastern traditions of meditation and yoga have become competitively marketed commodities – replete with superstores of profit-making accessories from instructional videos to yoga mats. In this culture, a culture not just of business but of manic busyness, meditation and yoga become merely another thing to do, to fit in to a busy lifestyle. Capitalist culture makes a fetish, icon or idol of everything that its marketeers seek to sell us.

Money is the supreme god of this culture, a culture of the commodity and of the market. And though money itself is a mere *immaterial symbol* (a dollar note would not be worth the paper it is printed on were it not for the curiously religious symbols printed on it) it is supposedly capable of miraculously transmuting itself into material things – commodities. Yet as we now see all too clearly, money itself creates nothing, despite the delusion that it can create something from nothing – even if only more money. The credo of the 'Monotheism of Money' is 'I am that I am' – or perhaps 'I am to increase what I am'.

Yet not only commerce but science too has its many gods. Thus physicists treat their own abstract, purely quantitative and wholly immaterial mental abstractions – the energetic quantum for example – as more real and fundamental than the tangibly experienced phenomena they are used to explain. Just as physicists worship an ill-defined entity called 'energy', biologists worship a no less ill-defined entity called 'the gene', and neurologists a lump of grey matter called the brain. Together they seek to reduce both consciousness and religion to a mere pattern of quantum fluctuations, a phantasm of the brain, or a means of evolutionary survival of the 'selfish gene'. It is high time, not to dispel 'The God Delusion' but its unquestioned counterpart – 'The Science Delusion'.

For again, before we can begin to question the truth or falsity of the belief that 'God exists' we must ask what exactly is meant by that word 'God'? Is it a mysterious 'force' or 'energy' – both ill-defined scientific terms? Is it a supreme creator being or a phantasm of the human brain, a construct of language or a means for the survival of genes? With this question in mind, the level of debate in the West about the existence or non-existence of God and the truth and value of religion is primitive in the extreme, centred as it is on an Abrahamic concept of god as a supreme being – one standing over, separate and apart from its creation and all other beings, in the same way that the human ego and intellect sees itself as standing over and apart from the human body and soul, and humanity has sought to stand over and apart from nature.

What all today's Western countless competing god-concepts have in common however is that their scientific or spiritual high priests seek to reduce God to some particular *thing or being* – whether in the form of a mysterious force or energy, a big bang or supreme being, Spirit with a capital 'S', or else person or trinity of persons. In doing so, they ignore the most fundamental question of all. How we know that any thing or being exists at all? The answer is simple. Only out of an awareness of it. The most fundamental scientific 'fact' or 'truth' therefore is not the 'objective' existence of a universe of bodies in space and time but a subjective awareness of that universe. We ourselves only know that *we* are or exist from out of an awareness of being and of other beings. There is only one possible conclusion we can come to from this fact. Namely that awareness – not just your awareness or mine but awareness as such – is the very essence of the divine – being a more primordial reality than any thing or being, force or energy, person or god, we are or could be aware **of.**

At this point I would like to cite the words of another Acharya – a great 10th century Indian thinker and polymath who has only recently come to be recognised as perhaps the greatest synthesist of Indian religious thought. His name is Abhinavagupta and his words read as follows:

"The Being of all things that are recognised in awareness, in turn depend on awareness."

In these words Acharya Abhinavagupta first expressed the basic truth of what I call 'The Awareness Principle'. For the first precept of this Principle is simply this – that awareness as such *is* the first principle of all that is, and not any things or beings, phenomena or experiences – whether natural or supernatural, physical or metaphysical, that, to use Abhinava's words, "are recognised in awareness".

Inseparable from this first precept of The Awareness Principle is a second one, namely that we cannot – *in principle* – reduce awareness to the private property or product of any thing or being we are aware of, whether the human brain or a supreme God-being. That is like attempting to explain dreaming by something we dream of. The very attempt to do so is absurd.

Let us say you dream of something or someone, anything or anyone – whether a speckled giraffe, a lump of grey matter, an angel or a 'son of God'. Would it be logical to argue that dreaming as such was the product or property of this one thing or being you dreamt of – that it was the cause of all dreams? Yet that is exactly what scientists such as physicists and neurobiologists explicitly do when they attempt to reduce not only dreaming but consciousness as such – what I term awareness – to the property, product or function of some particular thing we are conscious of, whether quantum fluctuations or the brain. It is also what religious believers do when they implicitly reduce consciousness to the private property of beings, whether human or divine.

Why should anyone come to such an illogical explanation of dreaming and of consciousness – one that reduces them to something we dream or are conscious of – and therefore does not in fact explain but already assumes the reality of consciousness? Only if they themselves are rather like sleepers caught in a dream – so unawake or unaware *that* they are dreaming, that they feel forced to seek an explanation for everything they dream of in some particular thing – or else in some intangible and unknown being in another world – the waking self and waking world of which they are unaware.

Hence the Eastern notion of spiritual enlightenment as a type of awakening – not from a dream but within a dream – the dream that we take as the rock-solid reality of our waking self and world. For as anyone with experience of *Nidra Yoga* knows – this being the yoga of dreaming and sleeping consciousness that is the theme of the next part of this afternoon's event – when we become aware that we are dreaming, an experience called lucid dreaming, that dream literally becomes more lucid – more clear and light-filled. That is because it is now permeated by the radiant light of *awareness* as such – that light without which nothing at all – not even what we perceive as physical light – would be visible at all. For all that we see and experience only comes to light in awareness – as a reflection and expression of the *light of awareness*. That is why when we speak of things 'coming to light' or of seeing or understanding them 'in a new light' these are no mere metaphors. That all this was recognised long ago in Indian thought is revealed by the words of Kshemaraja, a disciple of Abhinavagupta:

"Every appearance owes its existence to the light of awareness. Nothing can have its own being without the light of awareness."

Again, the expression 'light of awareness' is no mere metaphor transferring our experience of so-called physical light to the realm of the psychical. When we sense the brightness or radiance of someone's eyes what we perceive is the radiance, light or lucidity of *awareness* that shines through their eyes. This is nothing that can be measured in lumens with physical instruments. Indeed, as soon as we merely look at someone's eyes like an optician – as mere objects – we immediately cease to sense the qualities of awareness, light or dark, clear or confused, dead or alive, that communicate through the look *in* their eyes – for that 'look' is nothing objective but a mode of awareness – their way of looking out on and experiencing the world.

Different words shape and colour our awareness, and with it our way of looking out on and seeing the world – our 'world view'. This applies also to Eastern world views. Thus Buddhism speaks of enlightenment as 'awakening' – from the Sanskrit root *Budh*. Hinduism on the other hand emphasis 'liberation' or *Moksha*. Both have tended to emphasise the importance and challenge of individual spiritual awakening and liberation, whilst giving less attention to explaining the social and historical obstacles in the path of attaining it. The Awareness Principle on the other hand, allows us to identify clearly the biggest historical obstacle to both individual and *social* awakening and liberation. This is the core assumption – and accompanying experience – that consciousness is the *private property* of beings, human or divine. This idea has been entrenched in the human mind since the first types of society arose that were based on private property and ruled by property owning classes. Along with the idea of consciousness as the property of individual beings or 'subjects' went the notion that it is necessarily bound to particular material 'objects'. Marx again:

"… the representation of private interests … abolishes all natural and *spiritual distinctions* by enthroning in their stead the immoral, irrational and *soulless abstraction* of a particular *material object*, and a particular consciousness which is slavishly subordinated to this object."

This is not an affirmation of 'materialism' but Marx's decisive critique of it.

In contrast to the whole idea of consciousness as the private property of individual beings or subjects – and bound to particular objects – is the quite different understanding that can be found in Indian religious thought. This is the comprehension that all *individual* consciousness is but the individualised expression of a singular, *indivisible* and universal consciousness – one that not only takes the form of individual beings or 'subjects' of consciousness but also of all possible things or 'objects' of consciousness.

This universal consciousness is simply consciousness *as such*. It is because consciousness *as such* is both inseparable and yet at the same time wholly distinct from all specific *contents* of consciousness – from each and every thing we are aware *of* – that I prefer to use a different word for it – 'awareness' or 'pure awareness'. For to be 'conscious' in the ordinary sense is by no means the same as to be aware, let alone to *be* that very awareness. If people are engaged in thought or activities of any sort, whether making a cup of tea, talking to another person or listening to a lecture such as this, they may be conscious but they are not necessarily aware. To be aware is to be able, at each and every moment – to distinguish between anything we are conscious of thinking, feeling, saying or doing on the one hand, and, on the other hand, the pure awareness of thinking, feeling or doing it. It is this awareness alone that frees us from bondage – from what is effectively a quite unconscious identification with whatever it is we happen to be thinking, saying or doing, or however it is we happen to be feeling. That is why the great Acharyas of Kashmiri Shaivism identified awareness with one value above all – freedom.

This is also why understanding what I call 'The Awareness Principle' can lead – in itself – to a new awakening and liberating experience of pure awareness.

A word here about the word 'meditation'. We do not need to empty or clear our minds of thoughts and things to attain an experience of pure thought- and thing-free awareness through meditation. For what The Awareness Principle teaches is the simple understanding that the pure awareness of any thought or thing, since it is *not itself* a thought or thing, is already and *innately* thought-free and thing-free, just as it is also distinct from and free of any sensation, emotion or state of mind we might be aware of.

In Western thinking however, consciousness has long been identified, indeed defined by philosophers, as consciousness *of* something – a so-called 'object' of consciousness. Western philosophy has no concept of a type of pure awareness or consciousness distinct and independent from all contents or 'objects' *of* consciousness. This is rather like defining space as something that necessarily has contents – objects in it that we are conscious of – but not recognising the empty space around those objects and contents. Yet just as empty space is both inseparable from anything in it – and yet at the same also absolutely distinct from everything in it – so too is awareness both inseparable and absolutely distinct from all its contents, from everything we are conscious or aware of.

Space surrounds and pervades things, and yet it is not itself any thing in itself. Like space, awareness is also no 'thing'. And yet it is not 'nothing' – a mere spatial vacuum or void in which things happen to be. It is the other way round. What we perceive as mere empty physical space itself is nothing but the larger field or space of subjective awareness within which things first come to be and come to light.

Like both space and awareness, God too, is no thing. Yet nor is God merely one *being* among others, a being that just happens to have, own or possess awareness as its private property. The most fundamental religious truth that The Awareness Principle teaches is that God is not a being *with* awareness or consciousness. Instead, and quite simply; God IS awareness – not an awareness that is yours or mine, but one that is the very essence of the divine; not an awareness that is the private property of individual beings or persons, but an absolute, trans-personal and universal consciousness. Every single thing, from an atom or rock to a tree, planet or galaxy, and every type of being – animal, human or spiritual – is but an individualised portion and expression of this divine-universal consciousness. Note that I call this consciousness that IS God 'trans-personal' rather than *impersonal.* For, even though it is not a person, how can it be regarded as purely impersonal when it is the very source of our personhood – that which personifies itself as both gods and human beings?

An ancient and venerable analogy for this understanding of the Divine is the analogy of an ocean. An ocean is the *source* of all countless different life forms that arise and dwell within it – all of which are formed from the very substance of the ocean. Yet this does not mean that the ocean itself and as a whole has the nature of any of the life forms it gives birth to. It does not mean that the ocean is one enormous God-fish for example. Yet that is just what so many different schools of religious belief imply. These schools of religion can be compared to different types and schools of fish, each of which conceive their own ultimate or divine source – the ocean – as just one great big God-fish, albeit a fish of their own particular type of course – a great God-shark for example. They disagree only on what type of Great God-Fish the ocean is. Thus one religion may, on this analogy declare the ocean to be a Great God-Shark – but certainly not a Great God-Swordfish.

Clearly an ocean, just because it is the source of all fish, is *not* and need not be thought of as the 'mother of all fish' – a type of God-fish. Similarly however, though *all beings* arise from and within a divine ocean of awareness, this does not mean that *this* ocean, though the 'mother of all beings' needs to be conceived of as a single supreme God-being.

Today, religious belief in such a Big God **Being** clashes with the belief of physicists that the entire universe of Matter, Energy, Space and Time began with a Big Cosmological **Bang**. Yet 'Big Bang' cosmology is as logically flawed as Big Being or Big Fish religion or theism. For how can time itself be said to have begun with a dateable event *in* time? This elementary logical paradox seems to have passed our scientists entirely by. This only goes to show that science and physics, though it evolved from philosophy and metaphysics, has not only completely replaced philosophical and metaphysical thinking but lost all capacity for the most elementary logical questioning of its own language and concepts. That is why as the German philosopher Martin Heidegger noted: "Science IS the new *religion*."

A reporter once asked me (ignoring the reality of reincarnation) how I myself came to be a Hindu. My answer was not faith, belief or mere fascination with its symbols and rituals but something quite different – deep philosophical questioning, force of logic and direct religious experience. It was these that led me to both an understanding and an on-going experience of God *as* awareness – and as its manifestation in and as all things. I became a Hindu because I found this understanding that God IS Consciousness and that Consciousness is Everything – recognised only in Hindu religious thought and practice, in particular that of Acharya Abhinavagupta

113

and the religious philosophical tradition he renewed. In this tradition, refined and evolved in 9-12th century Kashmir, the divine universal consciousness was called by the name of a well-known Hindu god – Shiva. As a central scripture of this tradition, the *Shiva-Sutra* taught:

"Awareness – Shiva – is the soul of the world."

And in the words of Abhinavagupta's own guru Somananda:

"Shiva is ... all pervasive, quiescent awareness"

Hence the name of this tradition – Kashmiri 'Shiva-ism' or 'Shaivism'. The traditional name for *Shiva's* innate power of expression or manifestation as all things and beings is *Shakti,* which is also the name for the goddess or female consort of *Shiva. Shiva* and *Shakti,* masculine and feminine aspects of divinity were understood in Kashmiri Shaivism as distinct but inseparable aspects of the same singular reality, the same singular *awareness.* Since this awareness is irreducible to any thing we are aware of it is *transcendent* of all things. Since every thing is an expression of that, it is also *immanent in all things* – as their very *being.* This 'theology' of an awareness both transcendent and immanent is neither atheism nor theism, monotheism or polytheism, pantheism or panentheism. The only way of naming it in Western terms would be through a new term such as *nootheism* – from the Greek *'noos'* – meaning awareness.

'Nootheism' replaces monotheistic belief in a single supreme being with a monistic understanding of ultimate reality as a singular awareness. And yet it embraces both monotheism and polytheism, for that singular awareness comes to an awareness of its own being or selfhood through all the countless beings – human and trans-human – that arise within it. The gods truly exist, all of them and countless of them, each an individualised portion or personification of that singular or monistic awareness that is God.

As distinct expressions, personifications, portions or parts of that singular and divine awareness we ourselves are divine – we are gods. Being at the same time inseparable from that singular awareness as a whole – from God – we ourselves also are God. God is no-thing and no-being. Yet there is nothing and no being that is not divine – not a god and not God. Hence the *mantram* of Kashmir Shaivism – *Shivoham*. Translated this does not mean, 'I am God' – S*hiva* – but rather that 'God' – awareness – *Shiva* – is everything and everyone, including you, and me. *Aham*

From this point of view of all that I have said and indicated in this talk, I must admit to finding it deeply saddening that the leader and representative of a major Christian faith – one centred in this very city – should have referred to only one or two direct personal experiences of the divine. That is because for a truly devout Hindu, the divine is an ever-present, all-surrounding and all-pervading reality. It is that pure awareness (*Shiva*) whose power of manifestation (*Shakti*) is constantly coming to expression as all things and all beings – including the very walls of this room and all the people in it.

In this context, I would like to offer some words on what I call The Practice or Yoga of Awareness. Yet let me return to a basic precept of The Awareness Principle itself. Awareness, though distinct from anything we are aware of, also has the nature of an expansive and unconstructed field of consciousness, one that embraces far more than our normal consciousness. Ordinary consciousness, in contrast, is a highly focussed and therefore also constricted awareness. It is useful to consider this contrast in the light of Freud, who compared consciousness to a searchlight, like a torch light. A torch light, of course, is capable only of illuminating one thing or group of things at a time. Ordinary consciousness is like such a torch light, one that we move around in a more or less dimly lit room – focussing its beam now on this, now on that. In contrast, awakening to the spacious field of pure awareness is like switching on a light which illuminates the *entire* room, thus allowing us to be aware of far more things in the room at the same time – even whilst focussing our attention on particular things.

Right now and for the duration of this talk, unless and except for those times when your awareness might have drifted away in other directions, your awareness has probably been focussed on me and my words. You looked at me with your eyes and listened to me with your ears. Yet how aware were you at the same time of your breathing, of *your* body as well as mine, of your body as a whole and thereby also of yourself as a whole. And how aware were you at the same time of the entire *space* surrounding your body in all directions, the entire space of this room – and thereby also the bodies of all the things and people in it? Maintaining awareness of all-round space puts us in touch again with an expansive field or space *of* awareness. Identifying with that spacious awareness field is what allows us to transcend the narrow awareness spaces of our heads. The result is that we can literally 'take more in' – yet without feeling that our heads are getting filled up, our minds distracted or our bodies tiring – and without our awareness getting lost in any one thing, in any one focus or activity. Sensing all-round space also allows us to begin to breathe freely not through our noses but through our entire body surface – absorbing that all-pervading 'aether' of space (*Akash*) known as its vital air (*Prana*).

What I term 'The New Yoga', understood as The Practice of Awareness is essentially a movement from *Being Aware* – more aware and aware of more – to breathing the divine Bliss of *Being* that very Awareness. It is these three words, conjoined in the Sanskrit compound *Sat-Chit-Ananda* – 'Being-Awareness-Bliss' – that lie at the heart of Hindu religious thought, understood in a new and renewing way through the central precepts of The Awareness Principle.

RUDRA'S RED BANNER –
MARXISM AND MOKSHA

Introduction

The overall aim of this essay is to present a new trans-ethnic, trans-national, trans-sectarian, trans-Hindu and trans-Buddhist understanding of religious Tantrism and Advaitic philosophy – showing them to be complementary to secular European Marxism and Dialectical philosophy respectively. To begin with I contrast the opposing secular and religious concepts of 'liberation' signified by the terms 'Marxism' and 'Moksha', respectively – subjecting this apparently irreconcilable dualism to both philosophical and historical deconstruction, and showing the common understandings uniting Advaita and Dialectics. I then move on to stating the central claim of the essay, namely that the true locus of 'Moksha' – understood as *both* spiritual *and* political 'liberation' – is neither the body politic or community nor the individual in isolation but rather a 'third realm' identified by the Jewish thinker Martin Buber – namely that of immediate human relations *between* individuals in both social *and* communal contexts.

It is in this context that I argue that the essence of the Indian religious philosophy of Advaita or 'non-duality' is nothing but *relationality* as such – both between human beings, and between human beings and higher beings.

However in order to achieve a revolutionary religious transformation of relations between human beings (as well as between human beings, higher beings and God) I emphasise the importance of recognising differences or 'asymmetries' in levels of human awareness – yet without making the classic mistake of identifying these asymmetries with differences of gender, race, caste, class or culture. With such differences in mind however, the essay traces the subversive, sex-political dimension of religious 'Shaktism' and 'Tantrism' in colonial India, drawing intensively on Hugh Urban's research into the relation between British and Indian representations of their central symbol – the feminine goddess *Kali*. This leads into a discussion of more recent expressions of the sexual, political and sex-political dimensions of so-called 'left' and 'right-hand' traditions of Tantra in Europe.

Finally I draw on the work of Victor and Victoria Trimundi to show the historically misogynistic character of Tibetan Buddhism and Buddhist Tantrism in contrast to (a) the primordial Indian religious traditions of Shaktism, and (b) the synthesis of Tantrism in 'Kashmir Shaivism'.

In conclusion, I point to the future role allotted in the Buddhist *Kalachakra Tantra* to a figure called the 'Rudra Chakrin' – Rudra being, paradoxically, the Vedic god equivalent to Shiva, both 'Rudra' (Sanskrit) and 'Civa' (Tamil) meaning 'red' or 'reddening' – and *Chakrin* ('wheel turner') being a term synonymous with 'revolutionary'. The paradox is one of Buddhism itself raising the Red Banner of a Hindu god – Rudra – as that god empowered to turn the wheel of spiritual-political revolution for a coming age. However this 'red revolution' or 'inner revolution' as Robert Thurman (America's chief advocate of Tibetan Buddhism) conceives it, turns out to present only an amalgam of the weakest and least 'red-blooded' of liberal policies as its political platform for universal liberation or Moksha – policies totally empty of any Marxist understanding of capitalist economics, and sanctified and supplemented instead merely by the traditional Buddhist principle of "emptiness of self" and the advocacy of a new Tibetan-style monasticism.

In the first of three appendices, I cite from the Trimundis' critique of the idealised 'spiritual' image of social life in pre-Communist Tibet – an image still fostered throughout Europe and the West. In the second appendix I cite from Justin Whitaker's summary of the views of Marxist psychologist Slavoj Zizek on Western Buddhism. In the final appendix I cite a brief account of my own of the Virashaiva sect of Southern India, showing it to be an early example of a social-spiritual liberationary movement based on a tantric stream of heterodox 'Counter-Hinduism' long present within 'Hinduism' itself.

It is hoped that the essay as a whole may make some small contribution to a deeper and more thoughtful exploration of the secular-religious divide in India today.

Marxism and Moksha

'Marxism' and 'Moksha'. At first, the disparity signified by the two terms seems too great, the distance between them too daunting, the contradiction or 'duality' they signify too clearly defined to even warrant any deeper consideration – leaving us to accept without questioning for example, the unavoidability of the continuing political opposition in India between parties with a secular Marxist orientation and those based on a Hindu religious ideology. So let us begin by precisely setting out the distance and disparity between Marxism and its so-called 'materialism' on the one hand, and the spiritual-religious concepts of 'Moksha' or 'Mukti' on the other – doing so in the most seemingly irreconcilable or 'dualistic' of terms:

1. Marxism: a global secular, historical, atheistic and 'worldly' philosophy rooted in European thought and offering the prospect of liberation (the meaning of 'Moksha') and release from suffering only through a *social revolution* founded on the recognition and overcoming of *real* economic contradictions or 'dualities' in the world of *work*, in particular the unfreedom of the labourer in class

societies, an unfreedom deriving from that most decisive of all forms of alienation of the human being from the essence of his own being – what Marx called the "alienation of labour". For it *this* alienation, which, according to Marx, leaves the human being feeling most human only in the exercise of his most animal capacities (eating, drinking, fucking and herd-like 'partying' etc) and most *animal* in his most essentially human capacities – the God-like capacity for creative activity or 'labour'. In slave societies, the labourer as such is a mere commodity to be bought, sold and disposed of in any way by his master. In capitalism it is the individual's labour power and time – no less separable in essence from both their body and mind, that suffer the same fate – becoming a commodity to be sold and disposed of in any way dictated by capitalist owners of the means of production and *their* master, the Market.

The new modes of mass production developed with capitalism leave the individual's most individual creative potentials either unfulfilled or exploited – both in conditions of unemployment and even, if not above all in conditions of so-called 'full employment'. The two principle Mantra of Marxism can be spelled out as follows. In class societies life as creative sensuous activity is reduced to 'earning a living' – to *earning* a life – through a type of 'work'. Work in turn – and in its very essence is prostitution – the enforced economic prostitution of both body and mind on the part by the labourer in return for a more or less limited freedom to buy back its products in the form of commodities.

As Marx himself defined it:

"What then constitutes the alienation of labour? First, the fact that labour is external to the worker, i.e., it does not belong to his essential being; that in his work therefore, he does not affirm himself but denies himself, does not feel content but unhappy, does not develop freely his physical and mental energy but mortifies his body and ruins his mind. The worker therefore only feels himself outside his work, and in his work feels outside himself. He is at home when he is not working and when he is working he is not at home. His labour is therefore not voluntary but coerced; it is forced labour. It is therefore not the satisfaction of a need; it is merely a means to satisfy needs external to it. Its alien character emerges clearly in the fact that as soon as no physical or other compulsion exists, labour is shunned like the plague. External labour, labour in which man alienates himself, is a labour of self-sacrifice, of mortification."

This 'alienation' or 'estrangement' of labour, as Marx called it, "makes man's life activity, his essential being, a mere means to his existence." "Life itself appears only as a means to life".

No authentic state of 'spiritual freedom' ('Moksha') can be attained without the recognition of this, most fundamental economic form of spiritual 'bondage' – the economic *yoke* imposed on human labour. The idea of attaining such spiritual freedom merely through 'yoga' – a word whose root meaning is 'yoke', seems indeed, from this point of view, a mere cynical joke, compounded in our current era by the global commodification of yogic philosophies and practices themselves, which are marketed as a palliative for 'stress' – the individual's sense of alienation – whilst denying its foundation in economic exploitation. Such a commodified 'yoga' may serve to ameliorate, but thereby also serves to shore up the continuing yoke of alienated labour imposed by global capitalism, a yoke imposed not just on the free spiritual life of the individual but on their free bodily activity – the latter finding expression only through the compensatory euphoria of drunkenness or violence. This yoke can only be overcome through a communist social revolution.

2. Moksha/Mukti: the central spiritual aim of traditional, communalistic ethnic-Hindu religious philosophies rooted in India, yet conceived of, in contrast to Marxism, as an ultimate state of individual 'liberation' (Moksha) or 'release' (Mukti) from the entirety of worldly existence and the trans-historical cycle of death and rebirth. Moksha or liberation in this spiritual rather than social sense is seen as rooted in a recognition of the fundamental unreality (Maya)

of all apparent contradictions or 'dualities' of both thought and lived experience. It is attainable only through yoking oneself to specific mental and bodily disciplines or 'yogas' under the guidance of a guru, whereby the individual comes to a direct and sustained experience of the fundamental non-duality, non-separation or 'non-alienation' of the self from the divine – understood as a transcendent yet all-pervasive and universal reality immanent in all beings and manifesting itself at all times and in all epochs and life episodes – including whole historic epochs of conflict and conflagration, war and destruction, as well as individual lifetimes or episodes of suffering and violence.

Having thus set out in summary brevity, but I hope also sufficiently, the seemingly clear contradictions or 'duality' dividing and mutually opposing the secular and religious world-views condensed by the terms 'Marxism' and 'Moksha' respectively, the question immediately raises itself as to how this very duality is or might be understood within and from the perspective of each of these world-views. The question is a significant one precisely because both world-views are, in the most specific of ways, philosophies which, each in their own way, give immense prominence to the nature and relation of 'duality' and 'non-duality'. In the Marxist tradition, derived from Hegel, the key signifier of this thematic is the Greek-based term 'dialectics', and the notion of an immanent movement and evolution not only of thought but of reality itself, which takes the form of contradictions, antitheses or dualities progressively unfolding from one another in historical life through the emergence of a transcendent 'third' term – one which is no mere synthesis' of thesis and antithesis – for it no sooner arises than it becomes the first or 'thetic' terms of a new antithetical duality. In the Indian tradition it is the Sanskrit-based concepts of 'dvaita' (duality) and its counterpart ('a-dvaita' or non-duality) and the *duality and/or non-duality* of both that is the central, albeit de-historicised issue. One is reminded here of both Hegel, with his dialectical principle of the 'identity of non-identity and difference', and its advaitic equivalent – the non-duality of duality and non-duality. Before we stray too soon in the one-sided direction of either a dehistoricised or over-detailed historical analysis of both Dialectics and Advaita, let us first of all simply take note of their clearly apparent similarity (or 'similarity-in-difference') and the way in which, in and of itself, this implies a dimension of hidden 'unity' or 'non-duality' between 'Marxism and 'Moksha' themselves, an interstice of European and Indian thought that opens up a rich but still almost wholly unexplored vein of exploration – both philosophical and historical, religious and political. To begin with however, let us stick with the dimension of opposition and duality which the summary descriptions of the two world-views were intended to highlight – and simply tabulate, from the very words deployed in these definitions, some of the central linguistic dyads, dichotomies or dualisms they invoke:

MARXISM	MOKSHA
European	Indian
Social	Individual
Secular	Spiritual
Atheistic	Theistic
Modernistic	Post-Modern
Historical	Trans-Historical
Universalistic	Hindu Ethnic
Communistic	Communalistic

Paradoxically of course, the last dichotomy shows that Marxism is also and itself essentially a philosophy of liberation or 'Moksha'. The deeper purpose of this tabulation of antonyms however, is that it allows us to introduce a 'third term' besides the duality of Marxism and Moksha, but one of no little significance in relation to them both: 'post-modernism'. For those unfamiliar with the origins of this term, it is rooted in a model of language – both language as such and specific languages or 'modes of discourse' (not least philosophical, theological, scientific and theoretical languages) as more or less selective structures of mutually defining or opposing terms such as 'true' and 'false', 'black' and 'white', 'higher' and 'lower', 'good' and 'evil', 'positive' and 'negative', 'creative' and 'destructive', 'phenomenon' and 'noumenon', 'transcendent' and 'immanent'. Such dichotomies or dualisms, though they take the form of binary pairs or verbal distinctions need not necessarily be understood as contradictory opposites or antonyms. The specific theoretical language or 'discourse' of Marxism itself for example, though it revolves around a basic set of binary verbal distinctions or dichotomies such as 'use value and exchange value', 'base and superstructure', 'man and nature', 'idealism' and 'materialism', 'scientific' and 'utopian' socialism etc., understands each term as inseparable from its other – whilst the Marxist theoretical framework as a whole is precisely intended to serve the purpose of exploring the historical evolution and transformations resulting from their inner 'dialectical' relation. It is to this purpose that we owe Marx's historic analysis of the relation between the use-value and exchange value of a commodity. This begins on the level of simple barter of commodities, progresses through the simple market relation defined by the triadic formula 'C-M-C' (commodities being sold for money in order to purchase other commodities) and ends up historically with capitalist economies based on the formula 'M-C-M' – money invested in commodities in order to obtain a monetary return. At the same time the analysis of the commodity form in its dual aspect of use- and exchange-value, shows how the former use-value of things is progressively subsumed by and made secondary to their exchange value or 'market value'. Conversely 'exchange value' itself begins as the mere abstract idea of 'equivalence' between particular quantities of commodities with quite different material qualities and uses. Yet this abstract idea then itself takes on material form in the form of money – firstly in the form of precious metals such as silver or gold which retain their own use-value, and later in the form of mere materialized signifiers of exchange-value – 'paper money' with no inherent use-value of its own. With the increasing dominance of finance capital made possible through technologies of instantaneous global investments and divestments, exchange-value once again loses all material form and becomes a 'mercurial' quantity in the metaphorical sense – one whose sole reality is an ever-ex-changing 'virtual' reality flickering on the screens of stock analysts and traders in the world's great stock exchanges. The new formula of the inner relation of use-value in the form of the Commodity and exchange-value in the form of Money is now 'M-M-M' – for with the dominance of finance capital, exchange value in the form of monetary currencies and stock values itself become the principal Commodity, one whose sole use-value is its own increase and accumulation through financial speculation.

The deep historical dynamics revealed by such dialectical analyses however, is precisely the one which 'post-modernism' seeks to deny, arguing instead that it is not history but language as such – those very sets of binary constructs which make up the 'discourse structure' of particular theoretical models, world-views or philosophies – which themselves constitute or construct the very realities (including historical realities) that they claim to reveal or represent. The work of post-modern thinking then, is reduced to one of identifying and 'de-constructing' the binary constructs of any theoretical model or praxis – showing how they construct the very 'objects' whose true nature they claim to explain. Derrida in particular is responsible for this trend in thinking, one in which he particularly emphasised the way in which the language of any given world-view or theory tended to privilege one term or pole of a binary pair over its other – either by not naming its 'other' at all, or by treating it as less fundamental, real or essential. An example from Marxist theory would be its base/superstructure distinction – and the supposedly more fundamental and determining role allotted by Marx to the economic 'base' of society as against its cultural and political 'superstructure'.

Dialectics, Advaita and Deconstructionism

Applied to undialectical modes of religious, philosophical and scientific discourse however, the deconstructionist approach characteristic of post-modernism seems clearly vindicated. For it is only too clear how religious world-outlooks tend to invariably privilege or 'valorise' one pole of any given binary construct over another. Thus in the context of Judaeo-Christian religious discourse 'good' is clearly 'better' than 'evil', 'God' is clearly 'higher' than Man and Nature, the Judaeo-Christian God 'superior' to all previous gods (now spelled with a de-Romanised small 'g') and its theology 'truer' than all pre-Christian ones. Such a relatively simple (which is not to say simplistic) deconstruction of the languages of the Abrahamic religions (Islam included) is in no way as easy to apply to those of Asia and the East – Hinduism, Taoism and Buddhism in particular. For though they have an even clearer exposition of their own understanding of divinity as an ultimate or absolute reality, in the theological philosophies or 'theosophies' of all the 'Dharmic' as opposed to Abrahamic faiths we also find a more or less explicit counterpart to the Dialectical thinking so central to Marxism – hence what has come to be called Taoist or Buddhist 'dialectics', itself historically rooted in the Indian philosophy of 'Advaita' or 'non-duality'. Recognising this, we can begin to understand the very dichotomy or duality which is the subject of this work – 'Marxism' and 'Moksha' – on a deeper level, one which hinges on the meaning and relation not of two but of three distinct terms – 'Dialectics', 'Advaita' and post-modernist 'Deconstructionism'. The principal accusation levelled at the latter is one of totally relativising the truth of the different terms and distinctions that characterise different secular or religious world-views, since each not only construes but linguistically constructs the very concepts of truth or reality that it claims to singularly most truly represent. What this so-called 'post-modern' linguistic paradigm fails, paradoxically, to take any historic account of, is the way in which 'pre-modern' religious philosophies, Eastern and Western, were the first to acknowledge the formative power of language – whether as the Graeco-Christian concept of the 'Logos' or 'Word' become Flesh and the corresponding understanding of Nature as God's living speech, or both the Kabbalistic and Tantric theologies of a primordial alphabetic matrix of world-creation (Gematria/Matrika), one that Jews saw signs of in the Hebrew alphabet and Hindus in that of Sanskrit.

It is from the Greek word logos and its root verb legein (to gather) that the terms 'logic' and 'dialectic' itself derive, not to mention the '-logies' such as biology and psychology and common words as 'analogy', 'legend', intelligence, intellect etc. Indeed the abstractly theoretical term 'dialectics' can be understood in a more originary way through the word itself, and in particular through the common word 'dialogue', for this is a word whose root meaning has to do precisely with what is mediated 'through the word' (dia-logos). The word 'dialogue' however leads us into the realm of living human relations rather than abstract conceptual ones alone – what the Jewish social and religious thinker Martin Buber called the realm of the 'Between' or 'Inter-Human' (das Zwischenmenschliche). And what is mediated 'through the word', whether conceived dialectically or lived dialogically, can be understood as nothing less than relationality as such. Relationality in turn can be understood as the very essence, both of 'Dialectics' and 'Advaita'. For whether we posit a relation of duality or non-duality between any two or more elements, or even a relation of duality and non-duality, we still imply an initial set of elements whose relation is to be determined or posited as 'dual', 'non-dual', neither or both. Yet what if relationality as such is more primordial than any elements we seek to place in relation, whether a relation of separation or unity, duality or non-duality? What if relationality is what first distinguishes and unites the poles of any relation? What if, to use the expression of philosopher and physicist Michael Kosok, all identifiable or distinguishable elements of experience are not elements 'in' relation but of relation? In contrast, to simply posit or oppose a relation of duality or non-duality between any two things is to imply that they are not already dual elements or poles of a singular non-dual relation – like two sides of a coin. In this way we miss the essential point that 'duality' and 'non-duality' are themselves but dual aspects of relationality as such.

Relationality lies at the very core, not just of Dialectics but of Marxist theory as a whole, in a way which makes it entirely misleading in principle to think of it as a form of economic determinism, or even to describe it as 'social-ist' as opposed to individualistic. For one thing Marx's very definition of 'communism' was a stateless community in which "the free development of each is the condition for the free development of all" – and not the other way round as so many, not having read this definition in The Communist Manifesto itself, all too readily assume. More importantly, the primary aim of Marx's work from its earliest beginnings lay not in expounding some 'economistic' theory of society or individual consciousness, but rather in exposing how, in societies founded solely on economic property relations, relations between human beings are shaped by and ultimately reduced to relations between things – commodities. Similarly, as the Jewish thinker Martin Buber put it, the 'I-It' relation, a relation to some 'thing' or 'It' – or to the human being perceived as a thing or 'It' – replaces an authentic relation of beings, an 'I-Thou' relation. The relation of human beings to nature too, takes the form of an 'I-It' relation, thus reducing both human beings and nature to what Heidegger called a mere 'standing reserve' of exploitable natural or human 'resources'.

"In our age the I-It relation, gigantically swollen, has usurped, practically uncontested, the mastery and the rule.

The 'I' of this relation, an 'I' that possesses all, makes all, succeeds with all, that is unable to say Thou, unable to meet a being essentially, is lord of the hour."
Martin Buber

Revolution, Relation and 'The Third Realm'

So what can be done? If we wish to help bring about a revolutionary transformation of the world do we militate or meditate? Do we yoke ourselves to a socialist political ideology or to a spiritual guru, with neither or with both? Do we identify with modern, universalistic and revolutionary movements aimed at the realization of 'communism' or identify with a pre-modern, regionally-centred, ethnically-rooted and communalistic religion focused on individual self-realisation?

It was the profound insight of Martin Buber that the true locus of radical change or 'revolution' – the attainment of worldwide human liberation or 'Moksha' – lies neither in the realm of society or community nor that of the individual, that it can be achieved neither through social revolutionary movements – least of all nationalistic ones – nor through the security of self-centred religious or spiritual communities. Instead the decisive locus of revolutionary change is a third realm – one beyond the realm of the social or communal on the one hand, and the realm of individual consciousness on the other. The 'third realm' is the realm of relationality as such – of immediate human relations between individuals.

"The individual is a fact of existence in so far as he steps into a living relation with other individuals. The aggregate is a fact of existence in so far as it is built up of living units of relation."

Martin Buber

The starting point for a worldwide revolutionary transformation of human relations can only lie in immediate human relations themselves – in those very "units of relation" that shape the reality of both individuals and the social, economic or communal groups and institutions they belong to. 'Human relations' on a group, institutional, social, economic, communal, national, international and worldwide global scale can only be changed by changing the way in which individuals relate to one another as individuals within families and communities, groups and institutions.

No spiritual or political initiatives and activities can bring about any fundamental or 'revolutionary' changes in human relations unless those activities and initiatives are the expression of a revolutionary spiritual transformation of human relations between the very people who initiate them.

Raising each individual's awareness of the real economic, political and cultural contradictions that stand in the way of liberation or Moksha is the vital task of Marxism. Raising each individual's awareness to a higher plane *per se* – in a way that in and of itself can free individual consciousness from the yoke of these real contradictions is the task of traditional or classical 'yoga'. Learning to guard and embody this free liberated state of awareness (*Svatantrya*) in our living relations with other individuals in our life world is the task of a revolutionary 'New Yoga' – understood as a yoga of aware and transformative relating – a yoga of 'Relational Revolution'. Yet the sad but persistent dilemma besetting those on a traditional spiritual or political path is that the deeper or broader their spiritual or political awareness becomes, the more isolated they may feel – for example by finding relationships with those with different world-views or with a shallower or narrower awareness uncomfortably confining. As a result of this dilemma they may either retreat into deliberate isolation or else seek the superficial comfort of a group or community that merely shares the ideological or religious symbols of a 'higher' awareness. Deep or authentic community on the other hand can only arise out of living "units of relation" – multiple deep one-to-one relationships between its members. Such a community is quite different in nature from one that substitutes for such relationships – let alone one that suppresses them in the service of an overriding allegiance to a group ideology. That is why, in the absence of deep relationships and communion between specific individuals within a community, even such things as sharing in communal events – whether political gatherings or demonstrations or religious festivals and celebrations – may even end up leaving the individual with an intensified sense of isolation. Hence neither hermetic retreat, 'being alone together' in a symbolic community, nor resignation to what is felt as the compromise of 'ordinary relationships' may suffice to overcome the aware individual's sense of social isolation.

For the more politically-oriented individual this isolation may actually lead them away from aware relating to others and be replaced instead by a militant hostility towards others – for example in the form of individuals, groups or communities with other values or convictions, ethnic origins, class or colour. For the more spiritually oriented individual the same intensified isolation may lead to ever greater identification with their own divine Self – yet at the exclusion of aware relations to the living human Others in their lives. And whilst this can lead to the experience of evermore exalted and higher states of divine-spiritual Self-awareness, the individual's capacity to embody this awareness in deepened relations with a human Other diminishes. The result is a vicious circle in which an ever-greater spiritual 'realisation' of Self through relationship with God leads to an ever-diminished spiritual relationship to human Others. One very central reason for such dilemmas and vicious circles of isolation is a failure to fully accept and finds ways of responding to unavoidable asymmetries in adult-to-adult or peer relationships – differences in maturational levels of awareness. In peer relationships these differences may be felt by the more aware as isolating in themselves – or lead to them to act or be perceived as distant or haughty by the less aware. Parents or teachers, on the other hand, accept awareness asymmetries in relationships from the very start. They do not expect their children or their students to be cognizant or aware of all that they are aware. They not only 'make allowances' for their children's or students' lack of awareness, but relate to them with the aware intent to gently 'educate' and 'draw out' a greater awareness (e-ducare). This acceptance of asymmetry in the parent-child and teacher-student relationship comes to a different type of expression in the guru-disciple relation. For this is a relation in which the Guru unites the role of teacher with that of spiritual parent to another – albeit often younger – adult. The aim of the Guru in fulfilling this role however, is precisely to offer a model to the disciple of how they themselves can relate to other adults on a basis of total equality and respect, whilst at the same time acknowledging asymmetries or inequalities of awareness – not in order to accommodate to these, but rather to intentionally use

140

'skilful means' to overcome them – to heighten and expand the awareness of the other. This requires a deep capacity on the part of the Guru to meditate the other – that is to say to meditate and identify with a specific human other as well as with the divine self within them. Only in this way can the disciple be led to an experience of their own divine self – whilst at the same time learning from their Guru by what profound means and modes of meditative and aware relating they too can find relational fulfilment through spiritually teaching and parenting other adults.

Yet just as a child has only an inkling of the adult world of the parent, so the disciple has only an inkling of the larger world of awareness of the guru. And just as the child learns about the world of their parent in a way that is primarily relational – from the ways their parents relate to them from that world – so too, does the disciple learn about the guru's larger world from the latter's way of relating to them from that world.

What I have called 'The Awareness Principle' and 'The Practice of Awareness' constitute the grounding principle and practices of a 'New Yoga' – 'The New Yoga of Awareness'. Together they show how the false dualism of hermetic isolation and communal belonging can be overcome through practices of aware asymmetric relating. The Practice of Awareness in asymmetric human relations is based on The Awareness Principle itself. This 'principle' of awareness distinguishes all experiential contents of consciousness or awareness from consciousness as such or 'pure awareness'. The practice of this 'Awareness Principle' has to do with ceasing to identify with contents of consciousness – with anything we experience or are aware of – and identifying with the pure awareness of these contents. A central way of Practicing The Awareness Principle is to recognise that awareness of asymmetry – of the limitations, superficiality, lower level or narrower focus of another person's awareness – is nothing that need be felt or feared as isolating. Why? Because the very awareness of asymmetry is not itself anything limited, lowered, or rendered narrow or superficial by that asymmetry. The fear or discomfort of feeling one's own awareness confined within the narrower horizons of another comes from (a) fear or failure to be aware of asymmetry – to fully recognise, accept and make allowances for the limits or confines of another's awareness (b) failure to identify with the pure awareness of those limits or confines – an awareness that is not itself limited or confined by them, and (c) lack of the awareness and skills necessary to successfully relate to the other from a place of higher awareness – rather than feeling or being confined by the lower awareness of the other. If asymmetries of awareness are not responded to through aware relating, those with higher awareness may end up just avoiding social contacts, situations and relationships altogether out of fear of feeling confined and isolated by them. Without the meditative means to engage in aware relating in asymmetric situations, self-isolation is chosen as the safer alternative to social isolation.

Unavoidable asymmetries of awareness between individuals however should not be identified with differences of gender, class, race or caste. The belief that women and/or people of a different race or lower social caste or class are innately inferior in awareness has been the curse running through countless religions and spiritual traditions, Eastern and Western. It must be emphasised too, that awareness and acceptance of asymmetry in adult relationships, and the practice of aware relating in response to it, is not just a way of accommodating to the limits or lesser awareness of others. On the contrary, it is what allows the highly individual nature of the limitations evident in another person's awareness to become a source of deep interest, meditation, learning and insight rather than a cause for boredom or accommodation, restlessness or a sense of innate superiority. For the aware acceptance of asymmetries in relationships also turns all social situations into opportunities to recognise what I term 'reverse asymmetry'. By this I mean the opportunity to appreciate and learn from the unique individual qualities of awareness embodied or expressed even by persons with a 'quantitatively' lower level of awareness. The principle of reverse asymmetry gives expression to a notable autobiographical remark made by Martin Buber. Here he describes the enduring life inclination he felt impelled to embody, one which recognises both the transformative power of aware relating and the 'reverse asymmetry' or reciprocity of relational transformation. Thus, speaking of his central life inclination Buber wrote:

"It was just a certain inclination to meet people. And as far as possible, just to change something if possible in the other, but also to let myself be changed by him. At any event, I had no resistance…put up no resistance to it. I began as a young man. I felt I had not the right to want to change another if I am not open to being changed by him…"

These wise words echo the old Talmudic saying that a truly wise human being is one who finds something to value and learn from in each and every other human being. Aware relating is innately and intentionally educative and transformative, allowing the relation to teach and transform others – but only on the condition that one is open also to being transformed by it, above all by being open to and learning from the uniqueness of the other – what makes them different or 'special', however 'aware' or 'unaware' they are.

People have their own individual feelings and world-views, values and principles, fears and desires, dilemmas and problems, hopes and potentials. 'And' they have relationships, more or less fulfilling. The aim of a New Yoga of active and aware relating is to bring an end to this mere 'And', with its implication that relationships and relating are merely an appendage or optional add-on to our lives. Its aim is also to clearly distinguish relationships from relating. Relationships are something we 'have' or don't 'have'. Relating is something we do. So the fact that people may 'have' or 'be in' relationships, whether short- or long-term, is no guarantee that they relate to one another – let alone relate with awareness. Similarly, though people engage in all sorts of relational activities with others – whether educational or economic, recreational or therapeutic, social or even spiritual – this is no guarantee that they actively relate to one another in doing so. Relational activities are no guarantee of active relating. Then again, people are aware of having all sorts of everyday practical relationships with others – whether within the workplace, family, privately or as public citizens of state and society. But this too is no guarantee that they engage in aware relational practices – practices that are not a means to an end – even spiritual ends – but instead transform relating into a spiritual end in itself. For individuals can only sustain a deepened spiritual relationship to God through a transformation of the relational practices through which they engage with others – practices aimed at drawing out both the divine essence of the other and fulfilling the divine qualities and potentials at the core of their unique human individuality.

The Principles and Practices of Awareness that constitute 'The New Yoga' offer a wholly new dialectical and dialogical understanding of the essence of 'Advaita' or 'non-duality' – not as a more spiritual type of relation but as relation per se. They accord with Buber's understanding that the 'spirit' itself is no 'thing' but is our relation with a divine Other or 'Thou' – with 'God'. The principle of Advaitic philosophy is that we can come to experience this divine Other as a divine Self or 'I' within us, and within all beings – in every 'Thou'. The seeming dualities of 'I and Thou' or 'Self and Other' dissolve as soon as we recognise that both the divine Self or 'I' and its divine Other or Thou are but dual poles of a singular, non-dual relation. Buber distinguishes 'spirit' – which he understood as an inner relation to a Divine Other or Thou – from 'soul', which he saw as an inner relation to the world and other human beings. The 'self' that is ordinarily constituted by our everyday social relations is most often the ordinary 'worldly' or 'social' self consisting of what Jung called 'ego' and 'persona'. Yet what if our relation to the world and other people came itself to be centred in another self – that Self constituted by a spiritual relation to the Divine? In this way the duality of 'spirit' and 'soul', of the human being's inner relation to the Divine on the one hand, and to the world of individual human beings on the other, would dissolve. The two relations would themselves be experienced as dual aspects of a singular relation – that relation whereby the divine itself manifests as every 'thing' and 'being' in this world. This singular relation between God and World is one that can come to be experienced in and through the relation between any two human beings. Any such relation is in turn a 'bi-personal awareness field' which offers a portal to Other Worlds. Hence the famous saying of Christ – "where two or more are gathered…" In the specific Advaitic tradition known as Kashmir Shaivism, the Divine as such is understood as a dynamic relation between pure awareness on the one hand (Shiva) and its pure power of manifestation and embodiment in lived experience (Shakti). In contrast to the simple linear succession of life stages or 'Ashrama' of orthodox Vedic Hinduism – from student to householder or 'family man', and thence to community elder and renunciant hermit – the Trika or 'triadic' school of Kashmir Tantrism embraces the 'Kaula' principle of the soul family or 'Kula'. The Kula is itself triadic in principle – for it unites a threefold set of relations – the individual in his or her singular relation to the Divine, the Divine itself as a singular relation expressed in the relational unit or couple (Yamala), and the wheel (Chakra) of couples that make up the soul group or 'Kula' as such. Hence the words of Acharya Abhinavagupta:

"The essence of the tantras, present in the right and left traditions, which has been unified in Kaula, lies in Trika."

Political 'Left' and 'Right' in Tantra

Abhinavagupta wrote in the 10th century. In the immediate periods before, during and since the 20th century however, the terms *'right* and *left* traditions', used in connection with 'the tantras' attained a wholly new *political* connotation – or rather revealed in new and explicit forms many historically concealed political and social dimensions of those 'traditions'. Yet Abhinavagupta refers to 'the tantras' and not to 'Tantrism'. Though the tantras were seen as possessing an inner unity, the terms 'Tantrism' and 'Hinduism' both only emerged after the British colonization of India. 'Tantrism' was a word first coined only in the last quarter of the 19th century by the Sanskritist Monier-Williams, who identified it with 'Shaktism alone', associated with 'left-hand' cults of the divine feminine – and denigrated it as "Hinduism arrived at its last and worst stage of medieval developments". Yet as Hugh Urban so effectively argues in his book on *Tantra – Secrecy Politics and Power in the Study of Religion,* both 'Hinduism' and 'Tantrism' were not merely constructs imposed by a colonizing power but rather dialectical co-constructs of coloniser and colonised – both of whom sought to create unifying categories for the rich and diverse currents of Indian cultural religious history, indeed to 'imagine' India as such, and as a 'nation'. Tantra is for Urban an example of what Max Mueller long ago described as "that world wide circle,

148

through which, like an electric current, Oriental thought could run to the West and Western thought returns to the East."

Early Indian nationalism was a fusion of revolutionary anti-colonialism with religious symbols drawn from the tantras – in particular the bloodthirsty image of the great black Mother Goddess Kali – who became a symbol of the newly imagined Motherland itself in its struggle to violently purge itself of the demonic curse of white English goats or 'Feringhees'. Hence the early language of Indian nationalism:

"Rise up, oh sons of India, arm yourself with bombs, dispatch the white Asuras to Vama's abode. Invoke the Mother Kali. What does the Mother want? … A fowl or sheep or buffalo? The Mother is thirsting after the blood of the Feringhees. Chant this verse whilst slaying the Feringhee white goats: with the close of a long era, the Feringhee empire draws to an end, for behold – Kali rises in the East." Bengali newspaper 1905

Bipanchandra Pal

For the colonizers too, Kali was *the very image* of all that was terrifying, threatening, perverse, and abhorrent in the underbelly of Indian culture – uniting obscene idolatry and sexual license with organized political subversion and criminal violence of all sorts.

"To know the Hindoo idolatry AS IT IS, a person must wade through the filth of the thirty-six pooranus ... he must follow the Brahman through his midnight orgies before the image of Kalee." *William Ward* 1817

"One of the most pitiful of all the manifestations of unrest ... is the strange underground cult which has produced a secret bomb and revolver cult, an assassination society with secret initiation ...Behind all the cruelty and sudden death of the world lies Kali, the goddess of all horror ... Not even the perverted imaginations of the Marquis de Sade could devise a more horrible nightmare than Kali ... to minds such as students ... overstrained by premature eroticism ... this deity becomes a cult in which half-mystical murder may be a dominant thought." *MacMunn* 1933

In detail too thorough and extensive to summarise here, Urban shows how cults of the divine feminine or Shakti, united around the traditional tantric image of the mother goddess Kali as Chinnamasta (seemingly trampling on the supine body of her own god and consort Shiva) came to constitute, in Walter Benjamin's terms, a 'dialectical image' – "used not only to represent the humiliation of modern India but also to arouse revolutionary fervor and violence". He also shows how it was used to evoke a counter-image of the Bengali male as possessed of a powerful, warrior-like masculinity – in contrast to the English image of the weak and effeminate 'babu'. Paradoxically however, this very counter-image represented a *submission* to a Western concept of masculinity in diametric opposition to the traditional tantric identification of the divine masculine (Shiva) with 'Purusha' – a 'zero-point' state of pure awareness, absolute stillness and non-action – from and through which alone the boundless power (Shakti) of the divine feminine rises. It seems that this paradox was not lost on Sri Aurobindo, who, after withdrawing from militant, religiously-fuelled political activity re-established in his own life and philosophy the earlier tantric identification of the divine masculine with 'Purusha' or Pure Awareness, and of the divine feminine, personified by Kali, as a Pure Power of universal embodiment and manifestation. Aurobindo nationalist spiritual universalism counterposed the spiritual culture of India to the degenerate materialist culture of the capitalist West.

Such sentiments were echoed in the writings of colonial judge Sir John Woodroffe, alias 'Arthur Avalon', who sought to rescue 'Tantra' from the defamations of his British Imperial peers, arguing in contrast to Monier-Williams that – above all in the form of Tantrism – "India possessed a wonderful solvent, a solvent of irreligious materialism." Western civilization on the other hand was: "a great eater. We consume. What is called a 'higher standard of life' has meant that we consume more and more. Industrialisation, instead of satisfying has increased our Western needs. We want more wants." In a prescient anticipation of the economic 'rise' of India in today's global market economy he also warned that:

"India is now approaching the most momentous moment in its history ... The country will be subject to the play of monster economic forces ... the world-vortex ...Will she have the strength to keep her feet in it. I hope she may."

What he did not and could not anticipate at the time was that as capitalism continued its historic global march, it would begin to colonise, consume and then turn into marketable commodities the very spiritual traditions and teachings which others had relied upon to halt that march.

An early but notably strident affirmation of this tendency towards the commodification and consumerisation of 'tantra' can be found in several sayings of the 'neo-Tantric' guru, Acharya 'Osho' Rajneesh:

"The materially poor can never be spiritual."
"Capitalism has grown out of freedom."
"I *sell* enlightenment."

Rajneesh began his guru career precisely by speaking against socialism, and when he later discoursed on 'Tantra' he did so in a way that led it to be perceived as a mere form of liberated spiritual hedonism – 'aware indulgence' or 'sacred sex' – yet of a sort lacking any roots in the spiritual intellect and the profound theological comprehensions and practices of the Kashmiri Shaivite tantras.

In contrast to Rajneesh (1931-1990) the Marxist scholar Narendra Nath Battacharya (1887-1954) found in the history of the tantras "evidence for an archaic, class-free society, based on matriarchy and the power of the labouring classes – a system that would eventually be replaced by Brahmanical Hinduism and its patriarchal, class-based social order." (Urban) Battacharya emphasised that "Throughout the ages, the Female Principle stood for the oppressed peoples, symbolising all the liberating potentialities in the class-divided, patriarchal and authoritarian social set up of India … the success of Shaktism could not be checked because it had its roots among the masses."

His view was that India's primordial matriarchal culture was akin in nature to Marx's notion of an archaic form of communism. Within it 'tantra' was, according to Bhattacharya, more than a system of *spiritual knowledge*, for it also or above all offered the masses *worldly knowledge* in a broad range of areas of life and productive activity. Yet the very division between spiritual and worldly knowledge is a false dualism. For expanded awareness is the common source of *both* 'spiritual' inspiration, insights and intellectual comprehensions on the one hand, and intellectual intuitions related to practical 'worldly' activities and relationships on the other. Unable to integrate 'Marxism' and 'Moksha', Bhattacharya ended up retreating from Marxism into Humanism whilst at the same time never reaching for or attaining any feeling sense or experience of Religious truth.

Nevertheless, the use of tantric religious symbols as "weapons of insurgency or tools for revolutionary struggle" (Urban) continued. For meanwhile in Europe, two central figures – Mircea Eliade and Julius Evola – came to represent extreme right-wing exponents of the new Tantrism, held up as the sole tradition capable of providing a liberating counter-force to the irreligious degeneracy of Western 'modernism'. According to Eliade "It is only in modern societies of the West that non-religious man has developed fully … the sacred is the prime obstacle to his freedom … he will not be truly free until he has killed the last god." Yet like Battacharya – and indeed many other scholars of Indology – Eliade related Tantra to a "pre-Aryan popular strata" through which it "made its way into Hinduism". In contrast, Evola was no populist but an aristocratic elitist and 'conservative revolutionist' in the German sense, racist, but with a spiritual rather than a-biological concept of race:

"Tantrism may lead the way for a Western elite which does not want to become the victim of … experiences whereby an entire civilization is on the verge of being submerged." Writing of it as 'The Yoga of Power', Evola saw in Tantra a means for the de-emasculation of modern man – a path of heroic, free, individualist and elitist counter-revolution aimed at an emaciated Christian morality and an emasculated democratic and modernist culture. In his own words: "We may consider typical of Tantric speculation a metaphysics and theology of Shakti, namely of the principle of Power, or of 'the active Brahman'."

Noticeable is that all the figures we have mentioned so far identify Tantrism primarily with *Shaktism* rather than *Shaivism*, even whilst acknowledging, albeit to a greater or lesser extent, and with greater or lesser depth of knowledge, the Kashmir identificiation of divinity with *Shiva-Shakti*. This is something of great import in attaining a new and unified understanding of both the spiritual *and* political meanings of 'left' and 'right' traditions in tantra – with their double connotation of 'left-hand' and 'right-hand' on the one hand, and 'left-wing' and 'right-wing' on the other. For it was the left-hand tantric tradition that was associated with Shaktism, not simply as worship of the divine feminine but also with practices and rituals that incorporated physical intercourse, and in which paradoxically, the female tantric partner or Yogini could either play the decisive initiatory role herself – as guru – or else be reduced to a mere dispensable spiritual object and appendage for the male Yogin or Tantrika (such paradoxically misogynistic 'Shaktism' having been carried to extremes in Tibetan Buddhist tantric practices).

Whereas the practices of 'left-hand' tantra associated with traditional Shaktism culminated in a relation of outward bodily and sexual intercourse (Maithuna) between human partners – in a way that also left them more open to misogynistic perversion – the relational dimension of 'right-hand' tantra understood Maithuna as an experience of inner spiritual union or 'intracourse' *within* the individual between the divine feminine and the divine masculine. Paradoxically then, though *left-hand* tantra was associated with Shaktism and the divine feminine, in practice it often was seen and used as a means for the andocentric empowerment and liberation of the *male* rather than the female partner – hence its association with masculinist and politically *right-wing* practitioners. Conversely, it was *right-hand* tantra – which excluded in principle all possibility of misogynistic perversion in the service of male empowerment – had an intrinsically 'left-wing' political character. 'Shaktism' then is itself a deeply paradoxical or dialectical concept, for though 'Shakti' *means* 'power' or 'that which empowers' – the question has always remained 'whose power' and 'whose empowerment'? That of the male practitioner through spiritual exploitation of females, that of the female as initiatory guru or a truly mutual experience of 'awareness bliss' (Chitananda) attained through the male partner's identifying with the *Shaiva* principle of pure awareness and in this way liberating in the female partner the *Shakta* principle of pure power? In the era of feminism and sexual 'liberation' inaugurated in the sixties, it was all too easy to resolve this question by reducing the 'left-hand' path of Shakta Tantrism to some mutually heightened and supposedly spiritualised experience of *sex* – thus reducing the sensuality and sexuality of the soul (heightened awareness) to that of the body. Hence the now almost universal identification of Tantra, in both the popular mind and mass media, with 'Tantric Sex'.

As 'Tantric Sex' the Total Americanisation of Tantra has now become its complete 'Californication', both in name and effect a new 'Church of Tantra' aiming at nothing more than spreading and selling itself on the world-wide web. Thus, as Urban remarks:

"One need only enter the word 'tantra' into any good search engine to generate several hundred sites [a wild underestimation!] bearing titles such as 'Sacred Sex: Karessa, Tantra and Sex Magic', 'Extended Orgasm: A Sexual Training Class', 'Oceanic Tantra', or 'Ceremonial Sensual Pleasuring'."

The language of the example he cites is one of orgasmic 'doing it' and 'making it' rather than Awareness and Being. Its thought content can be compared to premature ejaculations of the adolescent mind, fuelling nothing more than fantasies of sexual gratification and economic gain:

"The Sex Magic Reality Creation Process is about maintaining one's focus during orgasm and channeling the energy into creating reality, any reality, whether it's creating a new job, car, experience, relationship etc. … What is your life like when you earn $85,000? What does it FEEL like? Make it big, in Technicolor … do whatever brings you to orgasm ..." *The Church of Tantra* website

'Kundalini' is reduced to a single mantra: "Juice it up, way up!" The 'it' to be juiced up here is clearly not the nectar or Amrita of the tantras – the serpentine, sensual bliss-substantiality of *pure awareness*. And since nothing is further removed from the divine- sexual dimension of the tantras than *biological orgasm*, the 'mantra' of this American 'Church' merely announces the global 'Coca-colonisation' of 'Tantra' as a religion of material success and sexual hedonism, one perfectly in congruence with the 'American Dream'. This is distorted 'left-hand' tantra of the most historically ignorant and politically *right-wing* capitalist type. We might well enquire then, what remains or has become, meanwhile, of the 'right-hand' tradition, and its relation to the socio-political 'left-wing' dimension of the tantras?

For as the right-wing advocates for Tantra, Evola and Eliade had reminded us – or rather warned us:

"We have now reached the last era, the dark age or Kali Yuga, which is a period of dissolution."

Julius Evola

"Humanity is fallen: it is now a question of swimming against the stream…"

Mircea Eliade

Yet whilst "… the *tantrika* does not renounce the world; he tried to overcome it while enjoying perfect freedom" the fact remains that "Against the terrors of history there are only two possibilities of defence: action or contemplation … Our only solution is to contemplate, that is to escape from historic time to another Time."

Stefan, in *Mircea Eliade*, The Forbidden Forest 1954

Such words are much more an affirmation of the 'right-hand' tradition, for they point to the trans-historical dimension of time into which true tantric meditation leads. This is the experience of Kali as the trans-temporal essence of time (Kala) itself, the circumscribing circle, sphere or womb of an *infinite time-space of awareness* within which our personal worldly concerns – and those of the current world at large – appear as transitory and diminutive in the larger scale of things.

The importance of deep metaphysical understandings of Tantra was emphasised by Agehananda Bharata, when he wrote that:

"Tantrism, like yoga and Vedanta ... could be respectable in the Western world, provided that the traditions of solid scholarship, of learning and intellectual effort ... did accompany their migration into the occidential world. Without these, I regard them as fraudulent."

Agehananda Bharata The Tantric Tradition

And indeed, in recent decades much 'solid' but intelligent and also sympathetic and feeling scholarship, particularly on the subject of 'Kashmir Shaivism', has found expression in the work of such leading figures as Muller-Ortega (*The Triadic Heart of Shiva*) and Mark Dyczkowski (*The Doctrine of Vibration*). Much is owed here to the pioneering work of Heinrich Zimmer on 'The Philosophies of India'. Born in 1890 and holder of the chair of Indian philology at Heidelberg University until 1938, he was forced to emigrate to Oxford by virtue of his marriage to a German-Jewess. As Urban records:

"Throughout his career, Zimmer's life and scholarship were intimately related: as his daughter recalls, his spiritual vision and his object of study were inseparable, fuelling him in a prolific search for meaning: 'life and learning for him were never separated. All his work was part of his life and his life part of his work'."

Like the scholars of head *and* heart that followed him he recognised in the tantras a *synthesis* of the Brahmanical intellect at its best with the "archaic matrilineal world-feeling of the aboriginal civilization of India." And though he never once set foot on Indian soil, through the "initiatiory ordeal" of the First World War, he also saw the contemporary significance of this synthesis, anticipating how – in our new modern 'Dark Age' or dark modern 'New Age', humanity "will tear to pieces the body of his mother, Nature, and will quarry her for new and different forms of power." However Zimmer's understanding of the metaphysics of Tantra as a historical synthesis (culminating in the writings of Abhinavagupta and the Trika school of Shaivism) contrast radically with earlier views, shared by both European scholars and Indian religious reformers such as Rammohun Roy, that Tantrism was the scourge of India, the source of her downfall, and a shameful degradation – "utterly devoid of every moral principle" – of the Aryan-Vedic religious tradition.

"If at any time in the history of India the mind of the nation as a whole has been diseased, it was in the Tantric age, or the period immediately preceding the Muhammedan conquest of India … Someone should take up … the diagnosis, etiology, pathology and prognosis of the disease so that more capable men may take up its treatment and eradication."

Benyotosh Bhattacharya

"… the purity of the race was soiled by marriage with native women … and the creed with foul Dravidian worships of Shiva and Kali, and the adoration of the *lingam*."

Isaac Taylor, The Origin of the Aryans, 1889

Such a view contrasted radically with the tantras revered in medieval India itself, not least the Kulanarva Tantra, whose hierarchical synthesis of religious doctrines and practices would later be adopted and crowned by Abhinavagupta with the Trika school of Kashmir Shaivism.

"Vedic worship is greater than all others. But greater than that is Vaishnava worship; and greater than that is Shaiva worship; and greater than that is Dakshinachara. Greater than Dakshinachara is Vamachara; and greater than Vama is Siddhanta; greater than Siddhanta is Kaula. Devi, this Kula is more secret than secret, more essential than the essence, greater than the supreme, given directly by Shiva, proceeding from ear to ear."

Kulanarva Tantra

What a contrast also with the words of Sir John Woodroffe:

"The full inclusion of the feminine element in public life will be the great fight of the immediate future … These circumstances, and the manner in which they are capable of being met by Tantra Shastra [Tantric Teachings] give another ground for the belief that this ancient scripture will become one of the religious influences of modern life, not … superseding Christianity, but in an interaction through which the Shakta Shastra will help … to produce a Mother-pearl of a complete and true religious exegesis."

Sakti and Sakta

Yet let us return to our central theme of 'Marxism and Moksha', and with it the quest for a revolutionary Tantra and 'Red Banner of Rudra' relevant to our own times. For historical scholarship alone, however thorough, sympathetic or even divinely inspired and devout (as exemplified by the life work of *Lakshmanjoo*) bears with it the danger of merely offering us a retreat to the religious language and traditions of an earlier historical era – thus not only evading Eliade's admonition "to escape from historic time to another Time" but also leaving us with nothing to say about *our* time, let alone providing a radically new and revolutionary direction for its transformation.

It is in this politically leftward direction that Urban points to the work of Gopinath Kaviraj (1887-1976), whom he describes as "undertaking a synthesis of the various Tantric traditions" similar to that of Abhinavagupta himself.

Yet as Urban stresses;

"Surely the most fascinating and original aspect of Kaviraj's system is his new vision of Tantra, which is now conceived as something far more than a quest for individual liberation. For Kaviraj, Tantra has the potential to achieve a collective salvation or universal liberation for humankind."

How Kaviraj believed this liberation might come about is summed up by the following citation from Arlene Mazak's dissertation on *Gopinath Kaviraj's Synthetic Understanding of Kundalini Yoga in Relation to the Nondualistic Hindu Tantric Traditions:*

"The *mahayogin* who has attained his own integral Self-realisation must look back compassionately upon all people sunk in their collective ignorance and dedicate himself to winning the integral Self-realisation of the entire world ... One *mahayogin*, working prodigiously within one lifetime, could eventually become identified with *paramashiva* as the imperishable *purusha* sleeping on the supercausal ocean. If this *mahayogin* could then awaken from the world-dream while still holding the physical body, the root ignorance in absolute subjectivity would disappear and the new kingdom of dynamic consciousness (*chaitanya*) would be created..."

Here we find a *trans-national* and *deeply esoteric* expression echo, in the late 20th century, the *national-political* message of the renowned 19th century visionary mystic Ramakrishna, who spent most of his life as a priest of Kali at the temple of Dakshinesvar.

"We must conquer the world through our spirituality … we must do it or die. The only condition of awakened and vigorous national life is the conquest of the world by Indian thought."

Yet it is *not* Indian thought that is currently seeking to conquer the world and overcome the 'non-Dharmic' or 'Abrahamic' faiths – Judaism, Christianity and Islam. Nor is 'Kashmir Shaivism' or 'Shaivist Tantrism'. Instead it is *Tibetan Buddhism* and *Buddhist Tantrism*. In this context it is interesting to note the resonance between the words of Kaviraj – and the role he allots to a singular 'Mahayogin' – and the Buddhist ideal of the compassionate Buddha or Bodhisattva as historic world-saviour and 'Mahasiddha'.

'Kashmir Shaivism', 'Tibetan Buddhism' and the 'Rudra Chakrin'

Returning to the apparent 'left-right' dualism of 'Shaivism' and 'Shaktism' we must note a fundamental distinction between Indian and Buddhist Tantrism. Indian Tantrism was rooted in worship of the Great Mother Goddess Kali. In the understanding of Kashmir Shaivism offered by The New Yoga, Shiva himself, *as* pure and absolute awareness *is* a constant meditation of the realm of undifferentiated potentialities *of* awareness which is the creative matrix or womb of the Great Mother. It is out of Shiva's meditation of the Mother, this being a pure *awareness* of the pure potentiality or *power* (Shakti) latent *within* awareness – that this at first undifferentiated power differentiates and manifests itself as countless *Shaktis* – emerging through the light of the One Supreme and Pure Awareness that is Shiva from the dark womb of the One Supreme Power or Shakti (Paramashakti) that is the Mother Goddess. Hence the opening sutras of Abhinavagupta's *Tantraloka*:

"May my heart throb, which is pure, seat of art, creative by the coupling state of Shiva and Shakti, Shakti (Mother Devi) who is creation, the cosmos and the divine mother and Shiva who … offers the internal bliss and external expansion…"

"I bow down to the deity Pratibha (Paramshakti) who is beyond, infinite and rests in the Supreme Awareness at the seat of the divine lotus situated in the threefold state beyond mind."

'Shaivism', understood in this way *is* the very essence of 'Shaktism'. In contrast there are forms of 'Shaktism' whose principle aim is not the recognition of the dynamic relational unity or non-duality of Shiva and Shaki – the divine masculine and divine feminine – but rather the *incorporation* of the latter into the former, of the feminine into the masculine. In their detailed research on this subject, available on the internet as an extensive text under the title 'The Shadow of the Dalai Lama', Victor and Victoria Trimondi argue that the very essence of both early Buddhism and the 'Diamond Vehicle' of Tibetan Buddhist Tantrism (Tantrayana) is 'androcentrism' – the *subjugation, subordination and sacrifice* of the divine feminine to the divine masculine. They themselves spell out their 'core hypothesis' as follows: "The mystery of Tantric Buddhism consists in the sacrifice of the feminine principle and the manipulation of erotic love in order to attain universal androcentric power." Rather than seeking to summarise the evidence they provide for this core hypothesis in all its historical detail, I will cite here only their own amplification and summation of its aims and claims, and the conclusion they draw from it:

1. The "sacrifice of the feminine principle" is from the outset a fundamental event in the teachings of Buddha. It corresponds to the Buddhist rejection of life, nature and the soul. In this original phase, the bearer of androcentric power is the historical Buddha himself.

2. In *Hinayana* Buddhism, the "Low Vehicle", the "sacrifice of the feminine" is carried out with the help of meditation. The *Hinayana* monk fears and dreads women, and attempts to escape them. He also makes use of

meditative exercises to destroy and transcend life, nature and the soul. In this phase the bearer of androcentric power is the ascetic holy man or *Arhat*.

3. In *Mahayana*, the "Great Vehicle", flight from women is succeeded by compassion for them. The woman is to be freed from her physical body, and the *Mahayana* monk selflessly helps her to prepare for the necessary transformation, so that she can become a man in her next reincarnation. The feminine is thus still considered inferior and despicable, as that which must be sacrificed in order to be transformed into something purely masculine. In both founding philosophical schools of *Mahayana* Buddhism (*Madhyamika* and *Yogachara*), life, nature, the body and the soul are accordingly sacrificed to the absolute spirit (*citta*). The bearer of androcentric power in this phase is the "Savior" or *Bodhisattva*.

4. In [Buddhist] Tantrism or *Vajrayana*, the tantric master (*yogi*) exchanges compassion with the woman for absolute control over the feminine. With sexual magic rites he elevates the woman to the status of a goddess in order to subsequently offer her up as a real or symbolic sacrifice. The beneficiary of this sacrifice is not some god, but the yogi himself, since he absorbs within himself the complete life energy[1] of the sacrifice.

If, as the adherents of Buddhist Tantrism claim, a logic of development pertains between the various stages of

Buddhism ... the relationship of the three schools to the feminine gender must be characterized as fugitive, supportive and destructive respectively. Should our hypothesis be borne out by the presentation of persuasive evidence and conclusive argumentation, this would lead to the verdict that in Tantric Buddhism we are dealing with a misogynist, destructive, masculine philosophy and religion which is hostile to life – i.e., the precise opposite of that for which it is trustingly and magnanimously welcomed in the West, above all in the figure of the Dalai Lama."

Victor and Victoria Trimundi The Shadow of the Dalai Lama www.trimondi.de

Despite taking this strong and hostile position, it is noteworthy that in their Postscript the Trimundis accept in principle the positive, life-affirming and revolutionary potential of a religious and political world view truly founded on the tantric God-concept of a divine masculine-feminine pair i.e., on a divine *relation* rather than a divine *being*, masculine or feminine. What they see as the disguised esoteric goal of 'Lamaism' – namely the *global establishment* of a *traditionally androcentric and misogynistic* Tibetan-Buddhist Theocracy or 'Buddhocracy' is at odds with the Dalai Lama's own assertion (which they cite) that an ideal solution to the world's problems lies in a synthesis of *Buddhism and Marxism* – and his critique of the *retreat* from

Marxism into crude capitalist materialism by the current, post-Maoist rulers of China.

Tibetan and Asian Buddhism and Tantrism were born from the womb of India's Vedic-Brahmanic culture. The chief question raised by the work of the Trimundis is whether this birth, like that of a distorted Christianity from Judaism, was, if not as a whole, then at least in part – a *deformed* birth – a misogynistic miscarriage or abortion. If so – and given the current Western 'fashion' for Buddhism and the consumerisation of diluted Buddhist 'meditation' as a palliative to the 'stresses' of capitalism – then the challenging task is of giving birth from Indian thought to a new 'Buddhism'. By this I mean a trans-Buddhist and authentically revolutionary form of global *tantric* religiosity and theocracy – not 'Buddhism' as we know it but a new 'Tantrism' beyond Hinduism, Buddhism and Taoism – remains the challenge of the day. It is *this* challenge that 'The New Yoga' is a response to. In this connection, and in the context of the title of this work, it is notable that in the *Kalachakra Tantra* – in essence the esoteric grand plan of Buddhist Tantrism to subvert and overcome the global theo-politics of the non-Dharmic or Abrahamic religions – a key role is played by a wisdom being called the Rudra Chakrin[2]. 'Chakrin' means 'wheel-turner' and is thus a direct synonym of 'revolutionary'. Given that Shiva is associated with the destructive Vedic god Rudra, the term

Rudra Chakrin is interpreted as wrathful 'wheel turner' or revolutionary. Yet this interpretation ignores the simple root association of the names *Rudra* and Shiva (from Tamil Civa) with ruddiness, redness or reddening. The *Rudra Chakrin* is, quite literally the 'red' or 'reddening' religious 'wheel turner' or revolutionary. Symbolically, it is a curious yet significant paradox that the *culmination* of the Buddhist Tantras should raise 'The Red Banner of Rudra' in its search to unite 'Marxism and Moksha'.

Yet any 'red' agenda of Buddhism in the Marxist or left-wing sense is totally belied by the spiritual politics of the Dalai Lama's chief American advocate, Robert Thurman. For in his audaciously red-covered book entitled 'Inner Revolution', he reveals a total lack of any Marxist understanding of the nature and innate contradictions of capitalist economics. The book ends up presenting a 'Political Platform Based on [Buddhist] Enlightenment Principles' which reveals his true political colours, boiling down as it does to a selection of the most yellow-bellied and tepid of 'liberal' policies of the sort which merely tamper at the edges of capitalist injustice (for example a 'revolutionary' proposal for graduated income tax, reduced military expenditure and the abolition of the death penalty). His political ideals and idealism do indeed centre on the idea of 'Moksha' as individual liberation. Yet this is watered down to a repetition of weak and outworn liberal *mantras* concerning the rights and freedoms of individuals – rights and freedoms of the sort long entrenched in the U.S. Constitution, yet which are denied in practice by the *de facto* power of the wealthy over the poor and the blatant, money-buys-power corporate plutocracy that is the true reality of U.S. 'democracy'.

Thurman's view of history is as naïve as his political 'platform' – opposing a Buddhistically Enlightened "inner modernity" in the form of Tibet's spiritual and religiously-motivated, monastic society[3], with the "outer modernity" of those secular, materialistically-driven and militaristic states that evolved in the West after the European Reformation and its 'Enlightenment'.

Thurman's vision of the *future* seeks only to combine the old Buddhist principle of "emptiness of self" with a revival of traditional monasticism. Yet no form of monastic education narrowed solely to the confines of any Eastern religious traditions, scriptures and philosophies can do them *true service* – revealing both the complexities of their inner relation to the history of *Western* philosophy, science and social relations – and their profound relevance for a *revolutionary transformation* of the latter. And "emptiness of self" is no recipe for what I have termed *relational* revolution. Only if 'emptiness' is understood as a pure, non-attached *awareness* of our own human self can it give rise to deep empathic resonance with others – and thus fulfil the much-vaunted Buddhist principle of 'compassion'.

Otherwise, the sole uniting factor between 'self and other' is "emptiness" itself and the term 'compassion' is emptied of all relational meaning. For as Buber emphasised, without an authentic Self or 'I' there can be no authentic relation to another as a 'Thou'. Through The New Yoga, the term 'authentic' is itself given a new and precise meaning – as both an *awareness* of our personal, human self in all its individualised and multi-faceted aspects and the recognition of its innate non-dual relation to a *divine, trans-personal Self*. The latter is that Self (*chaitanyatman*) recognised in the Shiva Sutras which, like the Divine, is identical with *awareness as such*. 'Enlightenment' from this point of view is not a negating 'emptiness' of self but an *affirming awareness of self* – an awareness identical with that Divine Awareness of which every being, not least every human being, is a unique living portion, expression and embodiment. It is through awareness and not "emptiness" of self, that, as Thurman writes "… the adept is always himself and the other at the same time", and thus a living embodiment of 'Relational Revolution'[4].

Notes:

1. The sexual dimension of The New Yoga as 'Tantra Reborn' is very far removed from the use of physical intercourse to drain what they call the 'gynergy' from a women in order to revitalise or empower a male yogin. On the contrary, it is about the use of pure awareness on the part of the yogin, identified with the pure awareness that is Shiva, to evoke and draw out the vital power of Shakti of the female partner or yogini – thus empowering her and transforming her into a living embodiment of the divine feminine. This is a sexual tantra of the 'soul body' and not the physical body. As such it transcends the dualism of left-hand practices based on physical body intercourse between partners and 'right-hand' practices based purely on a divine 'intracourse' of soul within the awareness of the solitary practitioner. (See *Tantra Reborn – on the Sensuality and Sexuality of the Soul Body* New Yoga Publications 2009)

2. "Let us return to the Rudra Chakrin, the tantric apocalyptic redeemer. He appears in … the epoch of the 'not-Dharmas', against whom he makes a stand …Before the final battle … the planet is awash with natural disasters, famine, epidemics and war. People have become ever-more materialistic and egoistic. True piety vanishes. Morals become depraved. Power and wealth are the sole idols. A parallel to the Hindu doctrine of the *Kali yuga* is obvious

here ... In these bad times, a despotic 'barbarian king' forces all nations other than Shambhala to follow his rule."

From *The Shadow of the Dalai Lama* Victor and Victoria Trimundi

3. Tibetan Buddhism, Buddhocracy and monasticism was and still is notoriously riven by sometimes violent sectarian conflict, dominated by dogmatism and spiritually educational only for a small minority. And like its counterpart – the celibate monasticism of military service – even if not compulsory, Tibet's spiritual rather than military monasticism was also economically enforced – by the sheer material poverty of its conscripts and their families.

4. See my essay entitled 'Relational Revolution' at www.thenewyoga.org and www.thenewsocialism.org

HINDUISM AND 'SCIENTIFIC SOCIALISM'

"I am a Socialist."
Swami Vivekananda

The Marxist philosophy of 'scientific socialism' is usually thought of as a form of crude, materialist philosophy, as suggested by terms such as 'dialectical materialism' and 'historical materialism'. That Marx's understanding of both 'materialism' and 'science' was in fact completely at odds with that of modern materialist science was made clear in his *Theses on Feuerbach*, where he writes:

"The chief defect of all previous materialism ... is that the object, actuality, sensuousness, is conceived only in the form of the *object* of perception, but not as sensuous human activity ... not *subjectively*."

The most basic scientific 'fact' of all – ignored in all modern sciences – is not the *existence* of a universe of perceptual objects, but an immediate subjective and sensuous *awareness* of such a universe. Since we only know of the existence of a universe, or of anything that exists, including ourselves, through *an awareness* of existing, it follows that awareness is – *in principle* – a more primordial reality than any possible thing or being that we are aware of. Put in other terms, *awareness* cannot – *in principle* – be seen as the property or product of anything we are aware of (including the human body and brain). Just as space cannot – in principle – be seen as something bounded by or 'produced' by any body in it, nor can awareness be seen as something bounded by or produced by bodies in space. Space itself is nothing 'objective' but the field or horizon of subjective awareness itself – unbounded by any phenomena we are aware of within it.

This principle, in a nutshell, is what I call 'The Awareness Principle'. The reason its radical and fundamental truth continues to be ignored is that 'subjectivity', 'consciousness' or 'awareness' has always been seen in Western culture and philosophy as the private property of separate, point-like human 'subjects' or 'egos', themselves bounded by the body or even mysteriously localised in the brain. Modern science is precisely a materialism of the sort that reduces even the human body and brain to mere *perceptual objects*, and then finds itself in the impossible situation of having to explain *how* such objects can miraculously give rise to subjective awareness. In this science of the human body there is no place for the human being, who is reduced to a phantom of the brain, a homunculus looking out at the world through the peepholes of the senses.

Yet what if all seemingly localised and point-like centres or 'subjects' of awareness are the expression of non-local *fields* of awareness or subjectivity?

What if subjective awareness is not a blank sheet on which we passively register sensory impressions coming from perceptual objects – but has its own innate sensuous qualities and patterns – for example the subjectively sensed lightness or darkness, colour and tone, levity or gravity of our moods, the subjectively sensed dullness or clarity of minds, the subjectively sensed size and weight, solidity or fragility of our bodies, or our subjectively sensed closeness or distance, warmth or coolness towards other beings?

What if such sensed qualities and patterns of subjective awareness *as such* are the source of all 'objective' energetic and perceptual patterns or 'gestalts'? What if 'the soul' is nothing supra-sensuous, insubstantial or disembodied, but is instead the bodily shape and form taken by such innate field-patterns and field-qualities of awareness?

What if the very substantiality of our bodies themselves is the sensed and sensual substantiality not of some material body or object of perception but of subjectivity or awareness as such?

What if all the sensory qualities of nature are the expression of 'soul qualities' – innate qualities of subjective awareness? What if these sensual qualities of the human being's soul nature can link us directly with the very inwardness or soul of nature itself? Then and only then, could we begin to comprehend Marx's concept of a *natural science of man* that is at the same time a *human science of nature*.

This will not be a crudely objectifying, materialist science of the sort we see today, but a 'subjective' or 'phenomenological' science – a science of immediate subjective awareness and experiencing. More precisely, it will be a 'field-phenomenology' of the sort articulated by the Marxist physicist and phenomenologist Michael Kosok in his seminal essay entitled *Dialectics of Nature*. For as he writes:

"Subjectivity, phenomenologically, simply refers to a field of presence, i.e., an immediate non-localised gestalt, 'opening' or 'awareness' whose content is constituted by events of mediation of determination – by 'objects' of awareness … Subjectivity, as a non-localised field of presence is nothing but concrete immediacy, i.e., experience as an on-going process, in which the events or event-complexes present are any objects, products or structures appearing out of the field … be they symbolic systems, physical objects or egos."

It is precisely this *phenomenology* of awareness between field and events which at the same time expresses itself as a *dialectic* of inseparable distinctions, or what in modern science is called a *non*-linear field of relations. In a dialectic relation, all elements are grasped as elements *of* relation and never simply as elements *in* relation."

In Marxism, as in Tantric Hinduism, revolution is seen as essentially to do with the liberation of the human senses and of human subjectivity – the soul – in its twin but inseparable or 'non-dual' aspects – as a transcendent *field* of pure awareness on the one hand and its sensual manifestation or 'contents' on the other. Unfortunately, with the exception of the tantric philosophies of Kashmir, Hindu religious thought and practices have been dualistically divided by those which emphasise and affirm the truth and validity of sensual experiencing and those which emphasise the field of pure sense-free awareness within which they arise. In contrast to Vedantic philosophy – which regarded sensual and bodily experiencing as essentially unreal, Tantric philosophy emphasises that pure awareness (*Shiva*) and its innate power of manifestation in sensual phenomena (*Shakti*) were distinct but inseparable aspects of the same Godhead or absolute reality known as 'Anuttara'.

Marxist 'dialectic phenomenology' shares with Hindu advaitic philosophy a recognition of this inseparability or 'non-duality' of the pure or 'transcendental' and the sensual dimensions of awareness. It also recognises pure awareness as having a universal, non-local or 'field' character – rather than being localised in individual beings or 'subjects'. As a result it is a 'subjectivism' in which subjectivity or awareness is not limited to or seen as the private property of the individual 'subject' or 'self'. It therefore avoids all solipsism, and with it the false philosophical question of how the self can come to know that others too have subjective awareness – the so-called question of 'other minds'.

"The so-called problem of the 'other' or of 'other minds' only appears if you think (Laing notwithstanding) that experience is private and in need of being communicated, i.e., that experience can be 'owned' like a commodity."
Ibid.

The way we 'privately' experience others is automatically sensed *by* others and vice versa. Subjectivity or awareness is in essence reciprocal or 'inter-subjective'. 'Scientific Socialism' is in essence a spiritual or 'Soul-Scientific' understanding of human relations – both to one another and to nature – one that recognises an innate unity between the souls of all being, not only with one another but with the aware inwardness or soul of apparently insentient 'objects'. Like Hindu understandings of subjectivity or 'soul', Marxism – understood as a science of subjectivity or soul – stands in radical opposition to all current forms of social and scientific reductionism, in particular what Marx saw as the reduction of the human senses in capitalist culture to the single sense of 'having', and the reduction too, of all immeasurable qualitative dimensions of human subjective experiencing to 'objectively' measurable and calculable *quantities*.

The failure to acknowledge the emphasis that Marx places on human sensuous activity as the *subjective* basis of human social life led to a false equation of Marxism with crude materialism and objectivism. What came to be called 'scientific socialism' was misinterpreted through the lens of capitalist science – which like capitalism itself, was based on the *objectification* of human beings and their alienation from their own subjective essence. Just as the concept of 'subjective science' is one totally absent in the vocabulary of so-called 'Marxists', so is the concept of 'Hindu Socialism' one totally lacking in the vocabulary of both secular Indian socialists and religious Indian Hindus.

What I call 'The New Socialism' is in effect a previously unarticulated 'Hindu Socialism' – for it conceives the individual 'soul' in a Hindu way – not as the localised product or private property of a skin-encapsulated self but as the expression of an infinite, universal and 'field' dimension of awareness – what Hinduism recognises as a *divine* dimension, indeed as the essence *of* the divine.

Only by distinguishing this pure, field dimension of *awareness* from each and every thing we experience within it – from all so-called contents or objects of consciousness – can we transcend and free ourselves from all those restrictive patterns of experience, thought and action that arise from a purely 'focal' awareness – one centred in a purely egoic and atomic idea of the individual subject, self or 'I'.

What Hindu yogis understand as 'God-Consciousness' or 'Transcendental Consciousness' does not come about through reflection – for all reflection on experience is itself part of the very flux *of* experiencing. Transcendental consciousness on the other hand, is essentially a pure *awareness* of experiencing, as distinct from any 'thing' we experience, or any particular mode of experiencing.

From the political perspective of the Transcendental Meditation movement:

"… when individuals experience transcendental consciousness, their individual consciousness becomes more coherent, contributing an influence of coherence to the collective consciousness of society, which in turn influences other members of society."

D. Orme-Johnson, Maharishi University of Management

Many forms of collective political action are not assertions of power but a reaction to feelings of impotence – arising as they do from the belief that as individuals we are powerless to influence mass events. From a field-theoretic perspective however, each individual's 'private' inner responses to mass events exerts a direct influence on mass events – reverberating within the mass psyche or the mass 'awareness field'. The subtlest of nuances in each individual's private inner feelings and 'position' towards actual or anticipated events will affect the course of those events – even if those feelings and that position are not formulated and spelled out, and whether or not they find expression in the public positions of political parties and spokespersons. Thus anyone who inwardly assents to an actual or possible war effectively promotes that war, even without voting for it or publicly voicing that assent. On the other hand, anyone who is aware of even the slightest feeling inclining them to assent to an actual or possible war – or to inhumanity of any sort – can, through that very awareness – choose to actively dis-identify with those inclinations and withdraw their inward assent.

"… any one-sided action is always a passive reaction to a given."

Michael Kosok *The Dialectics of Nature*

True individual freedom and political power come from awareness and not from political, action, reaction or mere analytic reflection. Truly effective action and truly deep political analysis have their source in *awareness*. Ultimately however, all forms of political action are always a reaction to existing patterns of action, whether in defence of, or in opposition to those patterns. Personal identity itself *is* a pattern of action. The struggle of progressive 'activists' against conservative 'reactionaries' is itself essentially reactionary politics in defence of one or other form of identity (whether ethnic, social, cultural or religious) based in turn on processes of *identification*. Like commercial advertising for commodities, the propaganda of political parties and leaders serves the purpose of enticing the individual to identify with a particular 'brand' of politics, and by doing so to bind their own personal sense of identity with its successful propagation or defence.

Just as Hinduism aimed at the transcendence of individual ego-identity, a 'New Socialism' – recognised in its essence as a type of 'Hindu Socialism' or 'Soul-Scientific Socialism' – would aim at the transcendence of all forms of *identity politics* through a politics of pure awareness. For pure awareness – including awareness of identity – itself *transcends* identity. A new politics of awareness would reveal the symbolic character of political events as the expression of contradictions not just in society but in the mass psyche of humanity and that of each individual, contradictions based on conflicting and unaware identifications.

HINDUISM AND THEOCRATIC SOCIALISM

"In humanity's evolution towards the ideal society the democratic order of ancient India, run on the principle of autonomous, self-governed polities, stands as an experiment splendid and unique. Sri Aurobindo considered *caturvarnya* [the four-caste model] to be a socialistic institution; inequality was external and accidental. He wrote that socialism (the solution to the economic impasse designed to concentrate on the inner progress of individuals) is essentially Asiatic and particularly Indian, and that democracy will never be fulfilled without it. Sri Aurobindo trusted that, by rediscovering the way to attune the world to Spirit, India will find the secret order for which socialism struggles. Turning humanity's most precious energies to its highest development, each member of the community exists for the welfare of all. *Sanatana Dharma* is the creed, God in humanity, humanity in God. He asked for 'the eternal religion' to be applied to contemporary politics, reshaping them into an ethical and spiritual pursuit."

Auroville Today

Early civilisations such as those of Mesopotamia, the Indus Valley and Egypt are also the only civilisations actually described by historians using the term 'theocratic socialism' – indeed it is only in the context of such civilisations that the term was first coined. Today the warning rung out to humankind through Marxism – 'socialism or barbarism' – has never rung more true. Except that we can rephrase it – a civilised *socialist theocracy* or a barbaric capitalist theocracy, the latter aided both by its chief ally (Zionist theocracy) and its chief rival (Islamic theocracy). A total collapse of civilisation and with it the self-destruction of humanity can only be averted through the building of a new and saner civilisation.

It was the entirely new knowledge, and the entirely new sciences – spiritual and technological – brought by the Sumerians to Mesopotamia, that laid the foundation of many of humanity's 'cradle civilisations' – including that of the Indus Valley. Today however, civilisation can only be saved and re-built – or rather a new and saner civilisation built – on the basis of new knowledge and new sciences – indeed an entirely new subjective understanding of 'knowledge' and 'science' as such. This new foundational understanding of the nature of knowledge is also the refoundation of a Hindu Tantric understanding of many diverse fields of both spiritual and practical knowledge – including science, medicine, education and economics.

Together these fields of knowledge, refounded as subjective sciences, could constitute the basic blueprints, building blocks, or 'foundation stones' for a new scientific and theocratic socialism rooted in Hinduism. What the Sumerians termed their 'MEs' (pronounced 'mays') and India civilisation called 'tantras' were practical spiritual-scientific blueprints, building blocks and foundation stones of this sort. Their 'spiritual-scientific' character lay in the fact that they were rooted in what 'subjective science' as opposed to so-called 'objective' science. 'Subjective science' means science sourced in inner, subjective knowledge and in subjective or 'phenomenological' research. Subjective science and research alone is true science and research – for it alone is rooted in a recognition of the essentially *subjective* nature of reality as such. The different fields and applications of subjective science are unified by a single principle – what I call The Awareness Principle. This radical principle of life, science and religion, rooted in Hindu religious philosophy, is the sole possible principle capable of uniting our understanding of social life, science and religion. It does so through the understanding that subjectivity or awareness is not a by-product of matter or the private property of any being – human or divine. Instead it is the divine source of all beings and all worlds.

Along with The Awareness Principle goes the recognition that 'God' is not a supreme being 'with' awareness. Instead God *is* awareness, an awareness that is infinite and unbounded – and not the private property of persons or of any of its divine personifications or gods. God is a 'multi-person' and more – each person's awareness being an individualised, living portion of the Divine Awareness. The expression 'God-Consciousness' refers to both an understanding and experience of God *as* Consciousness – an experience that must once again become central to the aims of social education and find renewed expression in social culture.

It is because The Awareness Principle challenges – like Hindu philosophies – the unquestioned dogma that subjectivity or awareness is the private property of individual persons, egos, selves or 'subjects' that it also challenges – and that in a much deeper and more fundamental way than ever before – the whole principle of private property on which class-based societies, whether dictatorial or 'democratic', have been based

'Socialist theocracy' does not in any way imply a lack of freedom or 'democracy'. We must remember too, that the modern term 'democracy' actually had its origins in the slave society of Athens – as democracy for the ruling class alone. Then as now, 'democracy' is in practice a form of oligarchy and plutocracy – a society in which only the landed or wealthy wield real political influence.

For true democracy, as Marx recognised, cannot be reduced to different forms of political democracy or democratic politics alone, but can only arise on the basic of an economic democracy or democratic economy of the sort totally lacking in capitalism – where not a single capitalist business or corporation is co-governed by its workers and employees, where not a single manager or chief executive is elected or accountable to those workers and employees. On the other hand these economically undemocratic or even despotic capitalist corporations wield, as 'interest groups' and 'lobbies', more effective power and influence than voters in the actual operations of political democracies and democratic politics.

In a true theocracy, the ruling priests and teachers, sages and seers are revered for their demonstrable knowledge and wisdom – not simply because they are voted into power through elections. As for democracy on the grass-roots level of the economy – the workplace – these need to be participatory and not merely electoral democracies. Socialist theocracy combines participatory economic democracy in the workplace with spiritual knowledge and leadership at the highest levels of the state and its institutions.

Today there is no such thing as a *non*-theocratic state – a state not ruled by an explicit or implicit 'god-concept'. Instead, every state is 'theocratic' – whether its ruling god-concept be Jahweh, Allah or Mammon; whether its prophets be Moses or Jesus, Mohammed, Darwin or Adam Smith; whether it be founded on the fundamentalist dogmas of monotheist religions, market economics or modern science and whether its high-priests are corporate managers, Islamic mullahs, Zionist zealots, or Christian missionaries.

National Socialism and Stalinism too, were theocracies – divinising the Nation and its Great Leader and combining materialist science with militarism and industrial feudalism or forced labour. Hitler's 'religion' was not some archaic form of Teutonic neo-paganism but biologism – supposedly 'scientific' medicine and genetics. His principal individual, social and political ideology was a form of 'New Age' health fanaticism – not only promoting vegetarianism and leading the first nationwide anti-smoking campaigns, but seeing Jews, gypsies and the 'mentally ill' as a dangerous genetic strain, infectious bacillus or tumourus cancer – threatening the 'wellness' not only of the individual but of the 'Volk'. His high priests were not the esotericist elite of Himmler's S.S. but renowned geneticists, physicians and psychiatrists.

To repeat – today there is no such thing as a *non*-theocratic state. Yet the grave civilisational crises we face today – economic, educational, ecological and cultural – cannot be seen as a result of a 'clash of civilisations' with their differing values and God-concepts. Instead this very clash is the result of an attempt to impose on the world a single religious monoculture – that based on the religion of capitalism – 'the monotheism of money' and its counterpart, the 'polytheism' of countless material commodities. The 'mission' of this religions is the use of economic and military power to ensure the transformation of the entire globe and all its natural resources – from genetic raw materials of life to water itself – into the most profitable commodities that can be made of them – irrespective of their affordability by the vast masses who cannot pay the price for them. It is the drive of capitalist theocracy for global dominance that now threatens civilisation as a whole with ecological, economic and nuclear catastrophes. And it is capitalist theocracy, centred in the United States, that can spend trillion of dollars on weapons whilst allowing 15,000 children to die each day of malnutrition and keeping billions in poverty through the abuse of its global economic power.

Whilst there is in essence no such thing as a non-theocratic state, it can equally be said that – aside from the pretensions of Iran and the ambitions of the Taliban, – there is no longer any such thing as a true theocracy in the traditional sense of this term – a society governed and guided by the genuinely knowledgeable or wise – as opposed to spiritually, philosophically, historically and culturally ignorant political 'leaders'.

The original theocracies of the past on which human civilisation itself was founded, not least Hindu civilisation, were not just socialist but 'gnostic' theocracies – founded on spiritual knowledge (*jnana* or *gnosis*) and not on military, political or economic might alone. Yet the knowledge borne by humanity's ancient ruler-priests or priest-kings was not *second-hand* knowledge of the sort that today's self-styled Christian, Islamists or atheistic scientists theocrats borrow from their Bibles, Korans or textbooks. Instead it was an in-born and intuitive bodily knowledge – genetically inherited from previous incarnations and/or genetically imprinted by their soul in the life between lives.

Today true science or knowledge – understood as subjective knowledge has given way to an identification of knowledge and science with objectivity. Today's objective' sciences seek to reduce all meaningful qualitative dimensions of human subjective experience to measurable objects or statistical quantities. Such is the bizarre mentality of these sciences that they would treat the purely quantitative measurement and models of the chemical constituents of oranges as more important and 'real' than any direct qualitative experience of their taste – as if the latter were 'merely' subjective. Such sciences are brought to the absurd position of having to invent absurd quasi-objective 'explanations' – whether genetic, evolutionary or neurological for basic subjective experiences such as love. In principle, modern science, far from being 'materialistic' or even oriented to perceptible objects is 'idealistic' in the extreme – seeing its own abstract scientific models and mathematical constructs as fundamentally *more real* than the perceptible objects and tangible, sensuous or emotional phenomenon they are used to 'explain'. Thus whilst no one sees 'light waves' or the energetic 'quanta' (photons) of which even the visible spectrum of electro-magnetic energy is supposedly made up, such invisible and immaterial realities are regarded as fundamentally *more real* than the actual experiences of light and colour they are used to explain. Far from being based on the innate evidence of the senses, science has long since sought to deny their reality unless 'proven' by some experiment to do with intangible, non-sensuous realities.

We are reaching the *reductio ad absurdum* of the equation of true knowledge with 'science' as is currently understood – the idea that such simple experienced phenomenon as the *wetness of rain* needs to be 'objectively' proven or explained in order for people to accept the evidence of their senses and their subjective reality. In a word, modern science is based on a dogmatic identification of scientific truth and reality with objectivity – despite the fact that there simply are no 'objects' independent of a subjective awareness and experience of them – an understanding long present in Hindu religious thought.

The doctrine and dogma of truth as objectivity means that today's purely quantitative sciences can give no account at all of such fundamental subjective realities as love or religious feeling – let alone 'explain' the origins of subjectivity or consciousness as such.

When Marx and Engels themselves coined the term 'scientific socialism' however, it was not this sort of 'science' they were thinking of. Nor was their 'science' a crude form of social or economic determinism.

For Marx, such economic 'determinism' merely reflected the capitalist status quo – a society in which the value of all values, including religious and ethical values, is measured only by their material and economic value. As for Marx's notorious denigration of religion as "the opium of the masses", its repeated citation completely ignores his broader project of rescuing human beings from all sorts of false gods – principally what he called the "fetishism of the commodity", "the monotheism of money" and the implicit worship of 'the market' – with its invisible yet supposedly benevolent and godlike 'hidden hand'.

Unlike figures such Lenin, Stalin and Mao, Marx did not seek political or state power of any sort. He was simply a brilliant teacher and thinker who offered human society a deeper knowledge of itself and of the dialectical laws – the *karma* – of its own history.

As the spiritual sage of "scientific socialism" aimed at overcoming crude materialist cultures and philosophies, he was, implicitly, a priest and prophet of a new 'socialist theocracy'. Both Stalin's 'Cult of the Personality' and

Mao's 'Great Proletarian Cultural Revolution' also had themselves a quasi-theocratic character – the former imposed from above by a supremely patriarchal ex-priest on what he knew was a deeply religious people, the latter being an extraordinary evocation of mass religious feeling on the part of a divinised Great Leader, and an attempt on his part to re-establish the democratic rural *commune* as the basis unit of both industry and agriculture.

In contrast, China today is an outright state-capitalist autocracy run by a 'revisionist' Communist Party of just the sort that the Cultural Revolution was launched to nip in the bud – but ended up fostering through the backlash against its excesses. Russia today is a neo-Tsarist capitalist autocracy run by ex-Stalinists – yet built on the backlash against the distorted Stalinist expression of socialist theocracy – the principle of which, again, only became so distorted because it was rejected in principle.

Yet whatever the dire consequences may have been of Stalinist of Maoist caricatures of 'theocratic socialism' or 'socialist theocracy', they only arose in practice from the very failure of crude interpretations of Marxism to accept the idea of theocratic socialism in principle. It was this failure that forced the hidden spiritual dimension of Marxism, and with it the unacknowledged spiritual needs of individuals in 'socialist' societies to come to expression in distorted ways – through *divinised dictators* able to recognise and exploit those spiritual needs for their own selfish purposes.

What is called 'theocracy' means a society governed by the power of the Divine. Yet the power of the Divine is not a power exercised *over* nature or human beings. For both human beings and nature are themselves a living expression *of* Divine Power or *Shakti* – of those infinite creative powers potentialities that emerge from womb of that great Awareness that is *Shiva*.

Sri Aurobindo believed in a future transition from capitalism, to socialism and thence to a type of 'communists anarchism' corresponding exactly to Marx's own definition of communism itself – as a society in which "the free development of *each* is the condition for the free development of *all.*"

"In the golden age or *satyayuga* there is no need for an external government: the self-determining individual and community live spontaneously according to their free, divine *svadharma*. This is the ultimate condition."

Auroville Today

Sri Aurobindo also recognised this future form of society would be characterised by a *subjective* rather than objective mode of rationality:

"The transition from the infra-rational (to which all the past political orders belong) to the rational age is thus complete, heralding the transition from the objective to the subjective, spiritual age. Then only the ideal of communistic anarchism can reach its full status: not just an ethical but also a spiritual perfection and the end of the quest."

MARXISM, HINDUISM AND INDIAN HISTORY

Introduction

Marxism is essentially an understanding of history which understands the fundamental dynamic of historical change as something rooted in changes in the technical 'means of production' – human beings relation to nature – and their consequent effect on what he called human 'relations of production' – in particular relations between those classes who owned the means of production (whether as slaves, land, or manufacturing capital) and those who did not.

Marxist economics is also based on a fundamental distinction between the *use value* of any product of human labour and its *exchange value*. It is only through processes of exchange – leading to the creation of money as a principal *medium* of exchange – that products of labour take on the principal character of exchange values ie. what Marx defined as *commodities*. In primitive and isolated tribal societies of the hunter-gatherer sort no surplus product for exchange was produced. In later forms of pre-capitalist economy such as slavery the human being himself became a commodity to be bought and sold on the market. And in feudal economies land itself was a commodity – the private property of a land-owning aristocracy.

Traditional forms of theocratic socialism took the form of cultures and civilizations founded on what Marx described as 'The Asiatic Mode of Production'. These were characterised by self-sufficient village communities or 'communes', each of which combined agriculture and craft manufacture through a well-defined hereditary division of labour which formed the basis of the *caste* system. They were neither slave nor feudal economies, since in the village commune land was essentially co-owned, and only its surplus product or labour took the form of an exchange value or commodity – becoming a vehicle of trade and of tribute to the state. The state also drew on surplus labour – either for the construction of great public works (for example irrigation systems or temples) or for war (military conscription in defence of common land).

The social-economic form of the village commune existed also in Russia and amongst Teutonic and other tribes of Europe – but endured much longer in Asia and in India in particular. It was the extraordinary historic durability of this system in India – its capacity to survive despite invasions, wars and countless changes of the ruling dynasties – that gave it an apparently *a-historical* culture – in contrast to those fundamental changes in socio-economic structure that lay at the heart of the entire history of Europe and the West. For there, propelled by new and more advanced modes of production, class and not caste came to dominate the social division of labour, though in the transition to capitalism both soldiers, household servants, the medieval guilds and Jewish usurers had a caste character. Yet European history was dominated throughout by class struggles between those who owned the means and resources of production (land or modern manufacturing tools) and those who, whether as slaves, serfs or labourers lacking their own independent means or production, were forced to surrender themselves or the products of their labour to them. Thus it was that in the capitalist system, farmers and artisans too, lacking large land holdings or modern industrial means of production were forced to become what Marx called 'wage-slaves' – having to sell their labour power to the owners of these means of production, thus reducing human labour itself to a mere *commodity* exploited for the generation of 'surplus value' and 'capital'.

Marx on India

Marx saw India – 'the Hindu economy' as a prime example of 'The Asiatic Mode of Production' based on the village community.

"… the Hindu [Indian], on the one hand, leaving, like all Oriental peoples, to the Central Government the care of the great public works, the prime condition of his agriculture and commerce, dispersed, on the other hand, over the surface of the country, and agglomerated in small centres by the domestic union of agricultural and manufacturing pursuits – these two circumstances had brought about, since the remotest times, a social system of particular features – the so-called *village system,* which gave to each of these small unions their independent organization and distinct life."

"Of the different forms of pre-capitalist societies, the Asiatic form necessarily survives the longest and most stubbornly. This is due to the fundamental principle on which it is based — that is, that the individual does not become independent of the community; that the circle of production is self-sustaining, unity of agriculture and craft manufacture, etc. If the individual changes his relation to the community, he modifies and undermines both the community and its economic premise; conversely, the modification of this economic premise — produced by its own dialectic, pauperization, etc. Note especially the influence of warfare and conquest. While, e.g., in Rome this is an essential part of the economic condition of the community itself [the armed defence of the land they cultivate], it breaks the real bond on which the community rests [by leading through military conquest to the enslavement of captives and the development of slave labour]."

"Those small and extremely ancient Indian communities, some of which have continued down to this day, are based on possession in common of the land, on the blending of agriculture and handicrafts, and on an unalterable division of labour, which serves, whenever a new community is started, as a plan and scheme ready cut and dried. Occupying areas of from 100 up to several thousand acres, each forms a compact whole producing all it requires. The chief part of the products is destined for direct use by the community itself, and does not take the form of a commodity. Hence, production here is independent of that division of labour brought about, in Indian society as a whole, by means of the exchange of commodities. It is the surplus alone that becomes a commodity, and a portion of even that, not until it has reached the hands of the State, into whose hands from time immemorial a certain quantity of these products has found its way in the shape of rent in kind. The constitution of these communities varies in different parts of India. In those of the simplest form, the land is tilled in common, and the produce divided among the members. At the same time, spinning and weaving are carried on in each family as subsidiary industries. Side by side with the masses thus occupied with one and the same work, we find the "chief inhabitant," who is judge, police, and tax-gatherer in one; the bookkeeper, who keeps the accounts of the tillage and registers everything relating thereto; another official, who prosecutes criminals, protects strangers travelling through and escorts them to the next village; the boundary man, who guards the boundaries against neighbouring communities; the water-overseer, who distributes the water from the common tanks for irrigation; the Brahmin, who conducts the religious services; the schoolmaster, who on the sand teaches the children reading and writing; the calendar-Brahmin, or astrologer, who makes known the lucky or unlucky days for seed-time and harvest, and for every other kind of agricultural work; a smith and a carpenter, who make and repair all the agricultural implements; the potter, who makes all the pottery of the village; the barber, the washerman, who washes clothes, the silversmith, here and there the poet, who in some communities replaces the silversmith, in others the schoolmaster. This dozen of individuals is maintained at the expense of the whole community. If the population increases, a new community is founded, on the pattern of the old one, on unoccupied land ..."

"The law that regulates the division of labour in the community acts with the irresistible authority of a law of nature ... each individual artificer ... conducts in his workshop all the operations of his handicraft in the traditional way, but independently, and without recognizing any authority over him. The simplicity of the organization for production in these self-sufficing communities that constantly reproduce themselves in the same form, and when accidentally destroyed, spring up again on the spot and with the same name – this simplicity supplies the key to the secret of the unchangeableness of Asiatic societies, an unchangeableness in such striking contrast with the constant dissolution and refounding of Asiatic States, and the never-ceasing changes of dynasty. The structure of the economical elements of society remains untouched by the storm-clouds of the political sky."

To identify the 'history' of India with the history of its kings and princes, generals and armies, battles, invasions and conquests – real or mythological – is therefore to miss Marx's point entirely. What lent early Indian history its essential and historically enduring character – its 'theocratic' and 'socialist' character – lay in it being essentially a property-less form of social organisation, one in which both land and natural resources were not regarded essentially as *either* the private property of individuals or the collective property of the villages but rather as something *granted* by a higher unity – the divine – as *embodied* in the divinely guided person of the ruler and institutionalised by the unifying functions of the *state*.

The king and state were not, as in European history, to represent and serve the interests of a property-owning or moneyed 'ruling class'. Instead the state *was* the 'ruling class' – or more precisely a set of 'caste' or 'castes' of rulers. In the words of D.D. Kosambi: "The *Arthasastra* state was not characteristic of a society in which some new class had already come into possession of real power before taking over the state mechanism" (1965, 143-4).

The question of caste

As the Indian Marxist economic historian Irfan Habib explains:

"Marx saw the Indian caste system as a special solution to the problem of the division of labour before the rise of capitalism. Outside of the village community – in towns or in the trade of surplus goods *between* villages – castes traditionally functioned as hereditary guilds. Inside the village community, where Marx understood there to be no commodity trade at all, castes functioned as an "unalterable division of labour" providing for those necessary crafts and services too specialized to be done in individual peasant households (and which therefore could not be supplied by the domestic "blending of agriculture and handicraft"). These service castes – the barber, the washerman, the potter, and so on, were "maintained at the expense of the whole community." So the caste system allowed each village to be self-sufficient, while at the same time maximizing the surplus that could be extracted in the form of rent by the state."

What then defined the *ruling castes* that constituted the theocratic *state* however? These emerged in my view as an over-arching extension of the village caste system – in particular through the elevation of *Brahmins* (teachers, scholars and priests) to a ruling religious caste guiding and protected by *Kshatriyas* (kings and professional soldiers), and making use of both *Vaishvas* (farmers, artisans and traders) and of *Shudras* (servant and service providers for the other castes). The division of these 'principal' four castes or *varnas* then became the over-arching 'caste system' overseeing what was in reality a much more highly differentiated and social division of labour including countless hereditary or non-hereditary, kinship, locality-based or even religious 'sub-castes' or *jati*.

According to Kosambi, in the establishment of the theocratic state, earlier communal deities, including matriarchal ones, were gradually incorporated into the Brahminical pantheon, resulting in the marriage of a primordial mother goddess such as Durga-Kali with a male god such as Rudra-Shiva. Among the Hindu religious schools, both Shaivites – worshippers of Shiva – and followers of the Tantras rather than the Vedas rejected all forms of caste discrimination and oppression – not least towards the lowest of the Shudra caste, the 'out-castes' or 'untouchables'. And both Indian history and religious mythology are replete with rulers and heroic figures associated with 'lower' castes. Yet not only Marx himself, but many Hindus recognise that the cultural rigidification of hostility and discrimination between castes severely weakened Indian culture – leading to the growth of class division and exploitation, making India less unified in the face of invasion, and making the lowest castes vulnerable to conversion – something no less true today.

The ancient Hindu economy and Hindu theology

Marx's analysis of the economic nature of the 'Asiatic Mode of Production' both reflects and explains the essential nature and origins of Hindu theology as a religion of *unity* or non-duality, not in the form of monotheism but rather a religious monism rooted in a state governed amalgam of autonomous communities or communes.

"Only in so far as the individual is a member – in the literal and figurative sense – of such a community, does he regard himself as an owner or possessor. In reality, *appropriation* by means of the process of labour takes place under these *preconditions,* which are not the *product* of labour but appears as its natural or *divine* preconditions."

"… the *all-embracing unity* which stands above all these small common bodies may appear as the higher or *sole proprietor,* the real communities only as *hereditary* possessors. Since the *unity* is the real owner, and the real precondition of common ownership, it is perfectly possible for it to appear as something separate and superior to the numerous real, particular communities. The individual is then in fact propertyless, or property – i.e., the relationship of the individual to the natural conditions of labour and reproduction, the inorganic nature which he finds and makes his own, the objective body of his subjectivity – appears to be mediated by means of a grant [*Ablassen*] from the total unity to the individual through the intermediary of the particular community."

"Part of its surplus labour belongs to the higher community, which ultimately appears as a *person* [a personified god, divine-king or priest-king]. This surplus labour is rendered both as tribute and as common labour for the glory of the unity.

"...irrigation systems … means of communication, etc., … then appear as the work of the higher unity ... Cities in the proper sense arise by the side of these villages only where the location is particularly favourable to external trade, or where the head of the state and his satraps exchange their revenue (the surplus product) … as labour-funds."

Ancient 'theocratic socialism' took the form then of a type of state communism or rather a state 'commune-alism' – one that allowed for the creation not only of great public works such as irrigation systems and mines, but also great cultural artefacts such as temples and a great cultural heritage. Cities did not come to serve, as they did in

Europe, as centres for the development of large scale manufacturing industry – employing wage-labour drawn from an exploited or landless peasantry, and destroying ancient arts and handicrafts. The destruction of rural handicrafts and creation of rural poverty only came about through English colonialism, the export of raw materials for industrial manufacture in England and the creation of a land-owning class on the English model.

"By ruining handicraft production in other countries, machinery forcibly converts them into fields for the supply of its raw material. In this way East India was compelled to produce cotton, wool, hemp, jute, and indigo for Great Britain. [...] A new and international division of labour, a division suited to the requirements of the chief centres of modern industry springs up, and converts one part of the globe into a chiefly agricultural field of production, for supplying the other part which remains a chiefly industrial field."

Now of course, globalisation has created a reversal or mirror image of this process – transforming Indian cities into centres for capitalist economic development and the manufacture of exportable commodities through the exploitation of cheap labour from the countryside, resulting in the ever-greater impoverishment of hitherto self-sufficient rural farming communities, and even in the mass suicide of farmers. Individual artisans no longer produce their wares or works of art for the use and value of their communities but rather as mere saleable commodities for a local and global market. It is in this way that the ancient theocratic socialism of India and Hindu religious monism have given way to capitalism and to 'The Monotheism of Money' – certainly the biggest and most backward social, economic and religious revolution ever to occur in Indian history. For as Marx himself noted, before capitalism made its inroads into India through the East India Company and the British Empire – leading ultimately to the disastrous division of India – all previous invaders, no matter how superior in military might, had found themselves unwittingly influenced – Hinduised – by the superior culture of their own 'conquered' subjects. Can the same happen again? Not through the recreation of an ancient Indian theocracy but only through the globalisation of a new Hinduism – one that does not oppose but *incorporates* the historical insights of Marxism.

References and further reading

Karl Marx *Pre-Capitalist Economic Formations*

Karl Marx *Capital*

Irfan Habib *Caste in Indian History* (1987)

Irfan Habib *Marx's Perception of India* (1983)

Suniti Kumar Ghosh *Marx on India*
Monthly Review, Jan, 1984

Prabhat Patnaik *D.D.Kosambi And The Frontiers Of Historical
Materialism* Prabhat Patnaik 2009

Dipak R. Basu *Marx and India* CiNii Annual Report 47
Nagasaki Universty

HINDUISM, NATIONAL SOCIALISM
AND THE INDO-GERMANIC CONNECTION

Historic Parallels

Just as India is divided by nationalist Hindu parties of the religious right and those of the centre and communist left, so was Germany divided between a National Socialist party claiming to represent the 'spiritual soul' of the people or *Volk* as a whole and Marxist parties claiming to represent the interest of the working class in particular. Whereas the Marxist parties sought to establish, through international revolution, the rule of the working class, National Socialism - in defiance of both Jewish and international finance capitalism and the atheistic 'socialism' of Stalin - needed to establish an authoritarian state in which a militaristic *ruling caste* (represented by the SS) served to protect the interests of the German people as a whole against British and American colonialism and imperialism and banking interests.

The National Socialists also lent political and military support to Indian nationalist leaders and movements in their struggles against English colonialism, they also adopted one of the most ancient Indian religious symbols – the *Hakenkreuz* (German) or swastika (Sanskrit *svastika* - meaning 'self-being') which also found throughout Iron Age Germanic and European culture. And just as Hitler foresaw the rise of a great Indian leader or *Führer* who would create a new Aryan empire governing the entire Asian sub-continent, so did certain Hindus – notably Savitri Devi – see Hitler as the world-saving *Kalki* avatar of the Hindu god *Vishnu*.

From a Marxist perspective, the terms 'National Socialism' or 'Social Nationalism' can be applied to all countries which nationalise or impose state control over their most important means and resources of production – not least oil production – previously exploited in colonial fashion by foreign-owned capitalist corporations. It was those 'National Socialist' or 'Social Nationalist' regimes in countries such as Indonesia and Egypt, and later also Iraq, Libya, Syria and Iran – which became key targets for 'regime change', first by the British, and then by Israel and U.S. imperialism.

Then again, not only did the National Socialists lend political and military support to Indian nationalist leaders and movements in their struggles against English colonialism, they also adopted one of the most ancient and sacred Hindu religious symbols – the swastika (Sanskrit *svastika*, meaning 'well-being') seeing it as representing the supposedly invaders – white, Nordic and 'Aryan' – who founded Indian Vedic civilisation. Hitler's connection and appeal to the soul of the German people appeared to lend 'National Socialism' the character of a Theocratic Socialism

– except that in its concrete and practical reality, National Socialist society was effectively a form of nationalistic and imperialistic *state capitalism* that merely embellished itself with a powerful religious aura whilst at the same time eliminating all genuinely *socialist* elements from both its party membership and political agenda. Hitler himself was first and foremost a firm believer in racial biology and technological science, and not 'socialism' or any religion, Eastern or Western. And the 'greatest' public works of the Hitler regime were not autobahns but concentration camps, industrial militarisation boosting the big manufacturing corporations – not to mention corporate built and manned by imported slave labour.

From a Marxist perspective, the term 'National Socialism' has a very different meaning to that which Hitler gave it – applying to countries which nationalise means and resources of production – not least oil production – previously exploited by private or foreign-owned capitalist corporations. It was those imperialist coups, assassinations and massacres which destroyed previously democratic 'National Socialist' regimes in developing countries such as Indonesia, Egypt, Iraq and Iran – installing corrupt, socially and politically oppressive dictators in their place – which first created the social and political vacuum that was later filled by radical Islam.

Esoteric and Exoteric History

The *svastika* symbol had long been used in German esoteric circles before its adoption and adaptation by Hitler - for example by the German branch of Theosophical Society which gave prominence to Indian religious philosophy. Behind this use of this symbol however, lies a lesser known esoteric history of the 'Indo-Germanic' connection.

Hinduism, as we know, recognises the reality of reincarnation, and yet few thinkers, Indian or European, have explored the esoteric relation between reincarnation on the one hand and exoteric history on the other, and the importance of reincarnation in coming to a religious-esoteric understanding of the relation between different historic cultures and civilisations. India, Greece and Germany may be regarded as the three richest and greatest philosophical cultures. And yet a most historically important example of the esoteric relation between reincarnation and exoteric history is the way in which the entire *soul of Indian religious philosophy* was *reincarnated* in Germany through a rich lineage of 19th and 20th century poets, linguists and thinkers associated with what is called 'German Romanticism' and with the different philosophical schools known collectively as 'German Idealism'. It began in the 19th century with figures such Friedrich Rückert,

Goethe and the Schlegel brothers. This Germanic lineage continued right through the 19th century into the 20th century through such figures as Arthur Schopenhauer, Friedrich Nietzsche, Paul Deussen, Jakob Hauer, Heinrich Zimmer, Edmund Husserl and Martin Heidegger. It also fed into esoteric schools such as Theosophy and Anthroposophy, as well as finding supreme aesthetic and cultural expression in the music dramas of Richard Wagner – himself a devotee of Schopenhauer. It attained self-understanding and self-recognition through Max Müller's discovery in Sanskrit of what appeared to be the oldest expression of a Proto-Indo-European mother tongue or root language, one still echoed in the pantheons of religious cultures as diverse as those of the Greeks, Nordic and Teutonic Tribes, Celts and Slavs all of whose languages have words and god-names cognate with those of the Vedas. The last and most important 20th century figure in the lineage of thinkers I have referred to was undoubtedly Martin Heidegger – who saw the type of purely instrumental, utilitarian and scientific rationality that had evolved since the Enlightenment as presaging "the end of philosophy" and its transformation into science – which he saw as *the* new religion – one which would entrench the global dominance of what he called "calculative thinking", thereby threatening the end of thinking as such – understood as "meditative thinking".

Germany as the India of Europe

Unlike their English imperial, military, commercial and colonialist counterparts, the lineage of German 'Romantic' scholars and thinkers *identified* with India and saw it as their spiritual 'motherland' or 'mother culture'. In doing so they attained a deeper self-understanding of the significance of their own specifically *German* spiritual culture, language and fatherland – recognising it as 'the Orient of Europe'[1], indeed effectively as 'the India of Europe'. Goethe in particular saw it as vital that Germans would not seek to establish a military-imperial 'nation state' on the model of England or France (and later America) but instead to recognise themselves as an essentially 'cultural state' (*Kulturstaat*). Many others saw the mission of Germany as that of guarding artistic and spiritual-scientific culture as such against the socially divisive and destructive effects of English industrial capitalism and the soul-destroying 'enlightenment' concepts of 'science' and scientific 'rationality' on which it was based. Even the very Kaiser who led a militarised German nation state into the First World War in 1914 saw this war as essentially a war to protect *spiritual culture as such* against the barbaric, crude and soul-less ethos of England commercialism, capitalism or 'Mammonism' – with its purely pragmatic and utilitarian 'philosophies'. This anti-capitalist and anti-English message was most famously expressed in a widespread propaganda tract[2] entitled *Händler und Helden* – 'Traders and Heroes'. This contrasted the English mentality of the 'trader' (*Händler*) with the German spirit of the hero (*Held*). Interestingly, this same message was spelled out also with reference to India: "This Germany cannot be defeated, nor can it be made to suffer the same fate as Hindustan. For today the world soul expresses itself through Germany." (*Schulze-Gävernitz*).

'Aryan Invasion' or 'Out of India'

There has long been a highly charged 'debate' between scholarly proponents of an 'Aryan Invasion Theory' (AIT) or 'Indo-European Migration Theory' – who locate the origins of Indian Vedic culture in central Eurasia, and the Kurgan culture in particular – and politically motivated nationalist proponents of an 'Out of India' theory (OIT) who see any migrations or invasions as having stemmed from the north-west region of South Asia itself – in other words a primordial Indian homeland. Genealogical evidence of all sorts – linguistic, archaeological and even genetic – is avidly sought, selectively sifted and brought to bear by proponents of both theories. The arguments on the part of ethnic Indian scholars however, no less than those of the objects of their critical attacks, are both based on a fundamental misconception of the true sources of sacred religious texts, symbols and cultures. Every form of

219

scholarly attempt to trace their historic and geographic source effectively denies in principle that their truest, most original source and homeland lies in the spiritual world itself and not in any geographical homeland or historical culture. Whether or not such texts reveal 'interlingual' or 'intercultural' elements – appearing to be translations of or containing words borrowed from other texts, languages and religious cultures, each of them is – first and foremost – the translation into language of a wordless 'inner knowing' or 'knowing awareness' (*gnosis/jnana*) that has its source, not in any earthly language or culture but in the spiritual world. And since what marks out all sacred religious texts *as* sacred is precisely their self-understanding as direct revelations from the world of spirit – from God and from the gods – there is no reason why any genuinely spiritually-motivated researcher, whether Indian or European, Asian or Western, Hindu or Christian, should either need or seek any form of linguistic, genetic, geographical or historical evidence of the primordial spiritual truths and sources of their religious culture, let alone lay claim to it as the 'private property' of their earthly homeland. To do so is to effectively deny its sources in the homeland of the spirit – the spiritual world – thus making its claims to spiritual truth and authenticity entirely conditional on scholarly analysis and 'scientific' evidence. Whatever regional or culture-bound forms or languages it may clothe itself in, spiritual truth is essentially universal, transcendental and trans-human in its source – it is nothing purely man-made. Nor, like some ancient scrolls or artefacts in a museum, is it the private property of a specific continent or country, language or religious culture, ethnic group or nation state·

The Divine Word and Divine Consciousness

Whatever degree of historic originality or primordiality they attribute to their own particular sacred languages (whether Sanskrit, Latin or Hebrew), many religious traditions also share in common an understanding of Language as such – and not any specific language – as something that is no mere man-made means of expression, but rather as the 'divine word' (*Logos/Vak*) and recognise the world itself as a living expression of that word – its living speech (*Brahmana*). The fundamental distinction between Language as such and pluriform languages, including 'sacred' languages, parallels the distinction between Consciousness as such (pure awareness or *Chit*) and pluriform individual consciousnesses that became so central to Indian thought. It also parallels Max Müller's distinction between Religion as such (understood as an innate religiosity or intuitive feeling sense of the divine) and specific, pluriform religions, together with his recognition that Religion as such – like Language as such – is the *a priori* condition for the evolution and diversification of specific religions and languages. This parallels the Indian

221

philosophical recognition that Consciousness or 'Subjectivity' as such – understood as identical with the Divine – is the precondition for all individualised 'consciousnesses' or 'subjects'.

Uniting the Indic and German Traditions

Today, the attempt to explain individual consciousness or 'mind' in terms of new quantum-physical theories has become the last-ditch 'scientific' defence against the rebirth of a metaphysical understanding of consciousness itself as that ultimate and universal reality it was recognised to be in the most refined schools of Hindu yogic and religious philosophy. This last-ditch defence of physics is wholly undermined and overcome by what I call 'The Awareness Principle' and its practice – 'The New Yoga of Awareness' – which, by drawing on the language and lineage of German thought[3], has succeeded in forging a new *body* of knowledge, one which is the self-conscious vessel for the reincarnation of the very soul of the Hindu religious tradition known as Kashmir Shaivism'. The New Yoga not only refines and evolves the basic recognitions upon which the traditional Hindu scriptures of Kashmir Shaivism are founded[4] – namely that the *atman* itself is identical with the light of that universal awareness (*chit, chaitanya*) that is *Shiva* – a light without which no suns and no phenomena of physical nature could be perceived, and no physical concepts of light 'energy' or 'quanta' could arise *within* awareness[5]. The New Yoga also integrates those two linguistically parallel recognitions that constitute the culmination of the Indian and Germanic traditions respectively – as lineages of thought:

1. The culminating recognition of the Germanic tradition that "Being is not a being" (Martin Heidegger) and thus irreducible to a supreme God-being, and individual being of any sort or a set or sum of such beings.

2. The culminating recognition of the Indic tradition that 'Consciousness is not 'a' consciousness' – that it is not reducible to a set of individual 'consciousnesses', 'minds' or to the property of an individual self or subject, ego or 'I'.

The New Yoga of Awareness is the Supreme Synthesis of these traditions, uniting them through the recognition that 'beings' as such are nothing but individualised portions and expressions of a singular, universal and divine consciousness, one whose essential nature is pure awareness (*Shiva*) and its innate potentialities or powers (*Shaktis*) of unbounded differential manifestation.

New Millennium Yoga

The question often asked is from what 'officially' recognised historical 'lineage' of recognised *gurus* the spiritual teachings of 'The New Yoga' derive. In response, it needs to be emphasised first of all that from an esoteric viewpoint, spiritual traditions and teachings are not dependent for their continuation on the temporal transmission of teachings through a historic 'lineage' of gurus and disciples. For just as the individual soul can reincarnate, finding rebirth in a different epoch, continent, culture and language – taking on a new and original shape through them – so can the soul of entire spiritual cultures, teachings or traditions. The 'New Yoga of Awareness is itself the reincarnation and rebirth, within a new epoch, continent, culture and language, after a gap of almost exactly one millennium and in the form of a new and original body of knowledge, of the very soul of the Hindu Tantric tradition known as 'Kashmir Shaivism' and that of all its teachers – independently of transmission in time through any lineage, and transcending any mere imitative reproduction, practice or scholarly interpretation of that tradition. This is its secret history, the source of its wealth of insight – and the challenge it presents to contemporary scholars, practitioners, gurus and 'lineages' associated with this tradition.

The misconceived need to see 'self-realisation', 'awakening' or 'enlightenment' as having its source in a temporal-historical *lineage* of gurus is directly paralleled by the need to genealogically trace a historic source or primordial homeland (*Urheimat*) for the diversity of Indo-European languages, cultures and religious scriptures and teachings – including the Vedas and Tantras themselves. In contrast to the German Romantics however, later ideologists reversed the belief shared by that lineage of thinkers who understood India as their spiritual motherland and Germany as 'the India of Europe'. Instead, and in line with the Aryan Invasion Theory, Indian Vedic culture was seen as the fruit of so-called 'Aryan' and Caucasian master race deriving from the North. On the other hand, Max Müller, the recognised German founder of Indology, still falsely associated with the 'Aryan Invasion Theory', declared quite plainly that: ".... who speaks of Aryan race, Aryan blood, Aryan eyes and Aryan hair, is as great a sinner as a linguist who speaks of a *dolichocephalic* dictionary or a *brachycephalic* grammar. Aryan, in scientific language, is utterly inapplicable to race. It means language and nothing but language, and if we speak of an Aryan race at all, we should know that it means no more than x + Aryan speech." [5]

From a truly Hindu point of view – one which accepts the role of reincarnation in history – religious cultures and philosophical teachings do only spread, diversify and evolve

225

through migrations and dispersions of peoples – whether from East to West, North to South – or vice versa. The essential weakness of both the 'Aryan Invasion Theory' and the 'Out of India' theory lie in substituting migratory genealogies with linguistic or spiritual-reincarnational understandings of the foundations of both Indic and Germanic culture – and their inner connection. This is also the essential weakness in the current Indian legal definition of what or who constitutes a 'Hindu'. Restricting this appellation to ethnic Indian or Asian Hindus not only goes against the Hindu doctrine of reincarnation, but prevents the recognition of Western Hindus as 'twice born' Hindus[7] in the reincarnational sense. And as we know, the true meaning of 'Arya' is 'noble' – not by virtue of birth or race, caste or class, but by virtue of *karma* and *dharma*.

Hitler and the National Socialists identified 'The Monotheism of Money' and its consequences with the Jews – both as a biological race and/or as a global *caste* of usurers and bankers with great influence on the nations they inhabited. Marx on the other hand, saw Christian and secular capitalist culture as the fully realised expression of the 'Jewish' Monotheism of Money, thus rendering its ritualised expression in the form of traditional religious Judaism both marginal and redundant.

Along with the emancipation of Jews that Marx described went an increasing degree of assimilation of Jews into their host countries and their identification with its culture – first and foremost German culture. The result of this was a continuing decline of Judaism both as a religion and as a homogeneous ethnic group. Zionism sought to combat this process, aided by the elevation of the so-called 'Holocaust' to the status of a new and unquestionable religion which could serve as a new foundation of both religious and secular Jewish identity. Nevertheless, the process of assimilation and acculturation managed to produce the phenomenon that Isaac Deutscher called "the non-Jewish Jew". Such Jews counted among their number such great and innovative thinkers as Marx himself (as well as Freud and Einstein, to name but a few) all of whom played a decisive role in creating modes of thinking, which like that of Marx, were in their own way subversive of both capitalism and traditional religious monotheisms.

If there is to be a renewal of Hinduism as a religious worldview – one that has, historically and economically, run counter both to Abrahamic monotheisms and to 'the Monotheism of Money' – then this renewal will most likely only spring from 'non-Hindu' (non-traditional and/or non-ethnic) Hindus.

References

1. See *The Orient of Europe: The "mythical image" of India and competing images of German national identity, 1760—1830* Nicholas A Germana, Boston College http://escholarship.bc.edu/dissertations/AAI3238828
2. *Händler und Helden - patriotische Besinnungen* Werner Sombart 1915
3. Wilberg, P. *Heidegger, Phenomenology and Indian Thought*, New Yoga Publications 2007
4. The Shiva Sutras 1.1 *Chaitanyatman* – 'Consciousness *is* the nature of the Self'
5. The words 'physics' and 'physical' are rooted in the Greek *physein* – to 'arise' or 'emerge'. Seers the world over, not least the *Rishis* who gave birth to the *Vedas*, did not invent or 'erect' a pantheon of supernatural 'gods', endowing them with arbitrary names. Instead they *sensed* these 'gods' directly in the sensual forces and phenomena of nature itself, seeing them all as 'shinings' (*devas*) of a suprasensual light – that light which the great sages of Kashmiri Shaivism recognised as nothing other than the *singular* all-illuminating and all-pervasive light of *awareness*– that light within which all things first arise (*physein*) and come to light' (*phainesthai*) as 'phenomena'. *"Every appearance owes its existence to the light of awareness. Nothing can have its own being without the light of awareness."* (Kshemaraja) *"The being of all things that are recognised in awareness in turn depends on awareness."* (Abhinavagupta).
6. Mueller, Max *India: what can it teach us?*

'Twice born' usually refers to Hindus who go through a ritualised re-birth ceremony inducting them into the upper three castes.

KRISHNA AND THE BHAGAVADGITA

The Jewish Torah or Judaeo-Christian 'Old Testament' clearly sanctifies genocide. Islamic fundamentalists claim that the Koran also justifies violent forms of holy 'struggle' or Jihad – at least in particular circumstances. A fundamental ethical question that needs to be raised also in relation to Hinduism – indeed any religion or ideology – is whether, as the *Bhagavadgita* appears to do, it too gives divine sanctification to war or violence, in contrast to Gandhi's stance that "There are many causes that I am prepared to die for, but no causes that I am prepared to kill for."

Gandhi stated the obvious truth that justifying national, state or communal violence whilst condemning individual violence was a contradiction.

"It is a blasphemy to say non-violence can be practiced only by individuals and never by nations which are composed of individuals."

On the other hand he did not fully explore the global political-economic and spiritual pre-conditions under which the practice of *Ahimsa* or non-violence could become universally viable.

The ethicality of battle and war is a central question in the *Bhagavadgita* – which has become perhaps the most well-known and most-read Hindu religious text and is seen by many as the 'bible' of Hinduism. In it, Krishna persuades the warrior-king Arjuna that his ethical doubts on engaging in battle with his kith and kin are unnecessary. In doing so Krishna uses the Hindu understanding that the Self is eternal and identical with *Brahman* – and therefore cannot be 'killed' – as a justification for war, rather than as an 'eternal truth' that, if heeded would render the very attempt to kill others redundant as well as futile.

Yet the *Gita* itself forms just one part of the larger *Marabharata* epic, in which questions of war, peace and the duties of the king as warrior or *Kshatriya* are explored through many different and conflicting voices and reflections, including pacifistic ones[1].

There have been countless interpretations of the *Gita*[2], including one by Gandhi himself in which he sees the battle in which Arjuna is about to engage as a metaphorical one – an inner battle of the soul. And in its final chapter, Krishna himself concludes his discourse to Arjuna by saying to him that "Having reflected upon it in its totality, do as you please." (18.63). Commenting on this, the interpretation of Abhinavagupta[3] is that "...the meaning of this statement is that the Lord instructs Arjuna not to think about the literal meaning (of this teaching) but the essence of it."

An important part of Krishna's teaching in the *Gita* lies in distinguishing the merits of previous, purely 'ascetic' yogas based on renunciation and withdrawal from social activities and duties from *karmayoga* – understood as disinterested action that is performed from a position of total indifference to its fruits, one that therefore does not employ rituals of a sort that seek to *utilise* a sacrificial relation to the gods for specific pragmatic purposes.

Arjuna's conflict between *kshatriyadarma* (the warrior's duty to fight) and *kuladharma* (duty to his own clan and teachers, which include the foes he is reluctant to kill in battle) is ultimately countered by Krishna through stressing the over-riding importance of *bhakti* – loyalty and to devotion to God – in relation to all other *dharmas*. Krishna's message is that only a king surrendered and devoted to God in the form of the 'Supreme Personage' of Krishna himself - and not a 'god-king' of the sort who regards himself as an overlord of the gods themselves and makes use of them as his instruments - can truly serve the well-being of his people. He can do so by restraining from despotic greed, indulgence and cruelty, whilst not renouncing the duties of office and caste – including his duties as warrior. The message is therefore also that all castes can find their way to ultimate liberation or *moksha* through the *karmayoga* of worldly action in accordance with their ordained duties or *dharmas* – a life of total *non-action* being impossible as long as one is incarnate. Persuaded by the argument that disinterested action does not bring karmic bondage – bondage to action or *karman* – and that even the acts of a warrior will therefore not bring negative karmic consequences, Arjuna duly goes into battle together with Krishna.

It is likely that Krishna himself was originally a clan hero who became elevated over time to the status of a supreme god. In contrast, Gandhi was a simple human being who embodied a quite different model of the socially active yogin or *karmayogin*. His message to the would-be warriors or *kshatriya* of his time was not one that sanctified war through the over-riding value and virtue of devotion, loyalty and sacrifice of ego to a single divine personage – but rather demanded of them a *sacrificial renunciation of violence itself* in fulfilling their duty or *dharma* of defending others. Along with this went recognition of both the heroic courage and the discipline or 'yoga' required to follow the principle of non-violence – thus offering a spiritual understanding of 'heroism' as a virtue and feat of the *soul* rather than the *sword*.

In the *Gita*, kingly devotion to the "infinitely superior force" personified by Krishna is at times presented both as a guarantee of military victory and as a way of avoiding karmic bondage through acts of war – so long as they were undertaken for non-egotistic reasons. This allows us to understand why some National Socialist ideologists could interpret the *Gita* as expounding an 'Indo-Aryan metaphysics of battle'. In its form as 'bhakti yoga' it found expression in absolute loyalty and selfless devotion to the supreme will of a deified Germanic clan leader - Adolf Hitler. The expansion of *Lebensraum* (literally 'life-space' or 'room for living') which Hitler wrote of in *Mein Kampf* became both a symbol and a substitute for an expansion of life-nourishing *awareness*. Notably, Hitler, like most Indians was also a strict vegetarian.

For this understanding to become a living social reality however, Gandhi constantly stressed how vital it was for believers in non-violence to feel that *"they had come into possession of a divine force or power infinitely superior to the use of the one they had"* (arms and violence).

Both Buddhism and Krishnaism evolved from within Hindu religious and cultural tradition, the former being, like Hindu Samkhya philosophy, an apparently 'atheistic' world view and the latter its mirror image – a type of pre- or proto-Christian Hindu 'theism' based on worship of Krishna. Yet within both contemporary Krishnaism and the Jesus-worship of evangelical Christianity there is a blurring or concealment of a fundamental distinction – albeit one acknowledged in the *Gita* itself as Krishna's 'secret'. This is the distinction between identifying God with a single divine *person* and the understanding of all gods and god-images as *personifications* of the divine in its ultimate, trans-personal dimension.

To some, the *Gita* appears to situate itself between the declining ritualistic 'polytheism' of the Vedas and the 'atheism' of Buddhist philosophy through a 'theism' which elevates Krishna to the position of supreme 'personage' of God. As a result, they see it as a model for a type of 'monotheism' that recognises other gods but places one god - in this case Krishna - above all others, elevating that god to the status of 'god of gods' or *devadeva*. This 'henotheistic' model would explain the rich plurality of mutually tolerant 'monotheisms' – each recognising others gods but each with its own supreme god (whether Shiva, Vishnu, Kali or others) that seems so characteristic of Hindu religious culture. And yet the Hindu henotheism of the *Gita* must be clearly contrasted with that of its European counterparts – for example the henotheism of the Greek and Germanic religions – which acknowledged no *trans-personal or transcendental* aspect of whatever god in their pantheon was held as supreme – whether Zeus or Wotan.

In the *Gita* on the other hand, what we find is less a type of classical monotheism or 'henotheism', but rather a model for what has been called 'vedantic' or 'advaitic' (non-dual) theism. This is essentially a *theism beyond theisms* – one in which in which *whatever* god is held as supreme is understood also as identical with the all-pervading source and essence of *all* things and all beings, human and divine – and not as dualistically separable from them.

For as is said in the *Gita*:

I am the source of the gods
I am being as well as non-being
I am the syllable Aum in all the Vedas
I am the enjoyer and the Lord of all sacrifices
I am the origin of all, and from me all proceeds
I am the life in all beings and the austerity in ascetics
I am the atman [self] seated in the hearts of all beings
I am the taste in the waters … the light in the moon and the sun.
I am the one who is to be known in all the shastras [teachings]
I am the consciousness in all beings

The 'I' that speaks here is neither that of an absolute or supreme being nor that of one god or being among others. Rather it is that *absolute consciousness* which is the essential self or 'I' of all beings. Seen in this light, the *Bhagavadgita* was and is a significant chapter in the continuing journey of Hindu religious thought towards a deeper understanding of its own 'eternal truth'. This truth lies in its radical essence as a form of *monism* transcending not only *monotheism* but all '-theisms'[4] (including atheism, polytheism, pantheism and henotheism) whilst at the same time embracing them all as valid sub-dimensions of divinity.

It is precisely this *radical essence* of Hindu religious philosophy which it has been the purpose of this book to both point to and help clarify. This essence unifies the five main streams or 'faces' of Hindu philosophy – Samkhya, Yoga, Vedanta, Advaita and Tantra. It does so through the Vedantic understanding that the 'pure awareness' (*purusha/chit*) recognised in both Samkhya and Yoga philosophies belongs to the very essence of both the Self and the Divine, and the Advaitic recognition that it is ultimately identical *with* the Divine –understood as an absolute and all-embracing awareness which is not only the essential Self of all beings but also immanent in all Bodies and the source of all sensuously experienced phenomena – the message of Tantra[5].

We are speaking here of a 'Godhead' whose nature is essentially nothing but a pure *awareness* transcending all gods, worlds, things and beings - yet whose timeless and constant *action* consists precisely of *godding* itself as countless gods, *worlding* itself as countless worlds, *thinging* itself as all things and *selving* itself as the essential self of all beings - thus *be-ing* their very Being.

References:

1. "Is there any beauty in war? Evil is this law of the warrior (Kshatriyadharma)...our law is like lawlessness ... It is well-known how the strong treat the weak, with contempt and violence ... The peaceful man sleeps easily because he has given up both victory and defeat."

2. See Angelika Malinar's *The Bhagavadgita, Doctrines and Contexts* for an excellent and detailed analysis of these interpretations from which I have drawn in this essay.

3. *Abhinavagupta's Commentary on the Bhagavad Gita (Gitarta Samgraha)* translated from Sanskrit by Boris Marjanovic, Indica Books 2002

4. "'Monotheism' and all types of 'theism' exist only since Judaeo-Christian 'apologetics'..." Martin Heidegger, *Contributions to Philosophy*

5. Specifically the Tantric philosophy of 'Kashmiri Shaivism' as expounded by Acharya Abhinavagupta and renewed for today's world in the form of 'The Awareness Principle' and 'The New Yoga'.

ABOUT ACHARYA PETER WILBERG

There are many who follow 'yogic' and 'tantric' practices derived from Indian religious traditions, just as there are teachers all over the world who seek to transmit the deeper wisdom of those traditions, and those who study and research these traditions as devoted scholars. Yet it is rare to find writings such as those of Acharya Peter Wilberg – which offer a new bridge between in-depth scholarly and philosophical study of such traditions on the one hand, and their exposition and experiential practice in different contemporary schools of yoga on the other. Fewer still are teachers and authors who do not merely write 'on' or 'about' these traditions, but instead are able to offer a wholly original contribution *to* them, intuitively re-conceiving both their philosophy and practices – and doing so from direct meditational experiences of a new sort as well as deep study and broad learning. Acharya Peter Wilberg is one of these rare few. That is why, amidst the mountains of literature and thousands of courses and websites on 'Yoga' and 'Tantra', the teachings of Acharya Peter Wilberg on 'The New Yoga' do indeed have something fundamentally *new* to say, not least about the very meaning of such basic terms as 'Yoga' and 'Tantra', 'Vedanta' and 'Advaita', 'Meditation' and 'Mindfulness', 'Prana', 'Kundalini' etc. That is because his aim has always been not just to share his own embodied spiritual awareness or 'inner knowing' but to crystallise it into a comprehensive new *body of spiritual knowledge* – one relevant not just to the life of the individual, but to our whole understanding of society, the sciences, religion and the future of human civilisation.

'The New Yoga of Awareness' is a body of refined 'yogic' knowledge built on the foundation of 'The Awareness Principle' and 'The Practice of Awareness'. It offers a wealth of new spiritual-scientific insights to all types of readers, whether familiar with traditional yogic and tantric practices or not, whether practitioners or teachers, scholars or philosophers, Hindus or Buddhists, Christians, Jews or Muslims. That is because Acharya Peter Wilberg, who understands himself as a "Tantric Hindu Gnostic Christian Socialist Jew", has reinterpreted the inner meaning of Eastern religious terminology, thought and practices in the broadest possible global and historical context. In particular however, he saw how his own unique inner experiences found their reflection in the different schools of Tantric religious philosophy known collectively as 'Kashmir Shaivism' or 'Shaivist Tantrism'. As a result he has been able to reinterpret this highly refined spiritual tradition on a new experiential basis and within a wholly new conceptual and terminological framework, one which he calls simply 'The Awareness Principle'. 'The Awareness Principle' and 'The Practice of Awareness' constitute the two inseparable aspects of 'The New Yoga of Awareness'. The New Yoga then, is an entirely new range of practices or 'Yogas' of awareness founded on 'The Awareness Principle'. Together they offer not only simple but profound life-principles for the individual to practice, but also powerful new forms of Tantric pair- and partner meditation. These are rooted in an entirely new understanding of 'tantric sex' (Maithuna) as the expression of a spiritual but highly sensual intercourse of soul – as *soul body* intimacy and intercourse.

The Principles and Practices of Awareness which make up The New Yoga of Awareness unite religion, psychology and metaphysics in a way that truly makes it not just 'a' new yoga but *the* New Yoga – effectively an entirely new and contemporary school of Tantra, and a rebirth of Tantric wisdom both *from* and *for* today's world. As such it has tremendous relevance *to* that world – not only scientifically and theologically but also for the psychological health of individuals, human relations and the world as a whole. That is because 'The Awareness Principle' provides a radically new philosophical foundation for our understanding not only of religion but of science and society. (see www.thenewscience.org and www.thenewsocialism.org)

It is the purpose of Acharya Peter Wilberg's writings to make this new Tantric wisdom known to the world in order that it can work *for* the world – reawakening in us all a recognition of that Divine Awareness which is the absolute or unsurpassable reality ('Anuttara') behind all realities. The nature of this Divine Awareness ('Shiva') and its immanent and autonomous creative power ('Shakti') was hitherto most clearly recognised in the Tantric religious philosophy of Kashmir Shaivism. Through The New Yoga however, the profound wisdom of this local and little-known historic tradition can now serve a much-needed contemporary global purpose – that of resisting 'The New Atheism' and the secular 'Monotheism of Money' that dominate today's world – along with the unquestioned assumptions of the purely technological 'Science' that is *its* new 'religion. In this way The New Yoga can help bring an end to the rising ocean of spiritual ignorance, and to the grave ecological devastation, economic inequalities and global mayhem that go with it. The New Yoga is a way of accomplishing this world-transforming aim not through Jihad, violence or war but through the supreme principle and innate power of Awareness. It makes known again that 'God' which is not simply one being among others 'with' awareness, but *is* awareness – an unbounded awareness that is the divine source of all beings, yet also immanent within them all as their eternal and divine Self.

A BRIEF BIOGRAPHY OF ACHARYA

Acharya Peter Wilberg is an Indian spiritual teacher reborn in North-West London in 1952 of German and German-Jewish parentage. Peter Wilberg's past-life and inter-life spiritual knowledge, psychic abilities and profound intellect came to expression in his early childhood – during which he already cultivated and practiced advanced yogic powers or 'Siddhis'. When only eight years old he spontaneously wrote an essay for his Religious Education class which expressed the essence of the Hindu-Tantric philosophy of time (Kaala), creative vibration (Spanda), and 'energy' (Shakti). Whilst still in primary school he practiced the yoga of dreaming – the ability to visualise and enter a dream directly from the waking state with his dream body – and retain full awareness within the dream. He also used daily classical music listening to cultivate a yoga of 'inner sound' and 'feeling tone'. This involved using his face and eyes as an instrument by which to express, embody and amplify the inner music of the soul – its tonal qualities of feeling. Later he assiduously cultivated a new 'yoga of the face' with which, simply by meditating the 'inner sound' of their look and facial expression, he could directly sense the inner feeling tones or 'soul' of another person within his own body.

Acharya Peter Wilberg first practiced the yoga of 'out-of-body' travel as an adolescent. Yet in early adulthood, whilst studying philosophy at Oxford's Magdalen College, he was a frequent invisible flyer over its quads. Whilst studying philosophy Acharya Peter Wilberg gave deep attention to Eastern as well as Western thought. His subsequent MA dissertation in Humanistic Psychology was an expression of his experience of the yoga of dreaming – being based on experiential research into inter-personal dimensions of 'lucid dreaming'. In his own lucid dreams he encountered numerous teachers and Gurus, travelled beyond our planetary system and experienced planes of awareness beyond the dream state.

This phase of his work culminated in a single dream which led him beyond the dream state itself into a deeper layer of awareness and a profound trans-personal experience of his own 'great soul' or 'Mahatma'. From within it he was wordlessly imbued with its higher knowing or 'Vijnana', as well as being instructed with his spiritual life-mission – that of re-conceptualising that knowing in new, more refined ways. Over subsequent decades he therefore continued to practice and seek new ways of articulating his many self-discovered Yogas, in particular that of using his face and eyes to mirror the looks of others and sense their souls – feeling their own soul in his body and his own soul in theirs. As a result, in 1975 he had the first experience of what was to become the new mode of

'Tantric Pair Meditation' that he describes in his essays and books – a form of tantric union or 'Maithuna' that he has now practiced for over 30 years. Through it, he cultivated his most important 'Siddhi' – the capacity, through his inner gaze and inner touch, to not only embody different qualities and faces of the Divine-Universal Awareness, but also to channel them directly into the body of another – the mark of a teacher with powers of initiation.

It was out of this rich history of continuous yogic practice and aware inner experiencing that Acharya Peter Wilberg was able to fulfil his life-mission and to formulate, over many decades, the original Principles and Practices of Awareness which make up 'The New Yoga'. In doing so, he has not only become the preceptor or Acharya of a new spiritual teaching. He has also become an empowered and initiatory 'Guru' ('Siddha Guru' or 'Diksha Guru') in the most traditional sense – capable not only of embodying Divine potentials and powers of awareness ('Siddhis') but also awakening them in others – thus bestowing initiation ('Diksha').

Together with his lifelong studies of both Indian and European philosophies, this extraordinary experiential history enabled Acharya Peter Wilberg to evolve, over several decades, the metaphysical principles and meditational practices which together make up what he calls 'The New Yoga' – a yoga of pure awareness (Shiva) and its innate potentials and powers of manifestation (Shakti).

Having a lifetime's study of profound European thinkers and philosophies behind it, The New Yoga is – in the most literal sense - a European 'reincarnation' of the sublime tradition of tantric teachings known collectively as 'Kashmir Shaivism'. For in the same spirit as its great 10th century adept and teacher – Acharya Abhinavagupta – Acharya Peter Wilberg has again, after a gap of ten centuries, further clarified and refined the principles and practices of this tradition. The New Yoga makes them profoundly relevant to today's world – capable of being applied directly in everyday life and relationships as well as to numerous modern fields of knowledge. That is why, in addition to his many essays and books on The New Yoga, Acharya Peter Wilberg has also contributed several articles to journals of philosophical psychology, written countless essays and published a variety of books on themes ranging from science and religion to medicine and psychiatry, politics and economics, psychoanalysis and psychotherapy.

BIBLIOGRAPHY 1

Other Books by Acharya Peter Wilberg:

Dreams, Music and the Many Faces of the Soul - *A Memoir of Metaphysical Experiences* New Yoga Publications 2014

The Awareness Principle – a radical new philosophy of life, science and religion New Yoga Publications 2009

Tantric Wisdom for Today's World New Yoga Publications 2009

Tantra Reborn – on the sensuality and sexuality of the soul body New Yoga Publications 2009

Heidegger, Phenomenology and Indian Thought New Gnosis Publications 2008

Deep Socialism – a new manifesto of Marxist ethics and economics New Gnosis Publications 2003

The Science Delusion – why God is real and science is religious myth New Gnosis Publications 2008

The QUALIA Revolution – from Quantum Physics to Qualia Science Second Edition New Gnosis Publications 2008

The Therapist as Listener – Heidegger and the missing dimension of counselling and psychotherapy training New Gnosis Publications 2005

From New Age to New Gnosis – towards a new gnostic spirituality New Gnosis Publications 2003

Event Horizon – terror, tantra and the ultimate metaphysics of awareness New Yoga Publications 2008

Head, Heart and Hara – the soul centres of West and East New Gnosis Publications, 2003

Heidegger, Medicine and 'Scientific Method' – the unheeded message of the Zollikon Seminars New Gnosis Publications 2005

See also:

Muischneek, Silya *The Awakening of a Devi – selected correspondence between Devi Silya Muischneek and Acharya Peter Wilberg*
New Yoga Publications 2009

Heinitz, Karin *Tantric Poetry – My Lord of the Living Light*
CreateSpace.com 2010

All books available from:

www.amazon.co.uk, www.amazon.com,

www.amazon.de and www.newgnosis.co.uk

INTERNET RESOURCES

www.thenewyoga.org
http://thesciencedelusion.blogspot.com
http://theawarenessprinciple.blogspot.com
http://heideggerindianthought.blogspot.com

BIBLIOGRAPHY 2

Abhinavagupta, *Sri Tantralokah* Chapters 2-4, translated by Gautam Chatterjee, Indian Mind 2008

Abhinavagupta *Abhinavagupta's Commentary on the Bhagavad Gita (Gitarta Samgraha)* translated from Sanskrit by Boris Marjanovic, Indica Books 2002

Attenborough, Richard (Ed.) *The Words of Gandhi* Commemorative second ed Newmarket 1982

Bhattacharyya, N.N. *History of the Tantric Religion* Manohar 1999

Buber, Martin *The Eclipse of God* Humanities Press International, 1988

Buber, Martin *Between Man and Man,* Routledge Classics 2002

Buber, Martin *I and Thou* T&T Clark 1996

Chatterjee, Margaret *Contemporary Indian Philosophy* Motilal Banarsidass 1998

Coburn, Thomas B. *Devi Mahatmya* Motilal 2002

Dupoche, John R. *Abhinavagupta – The Kula Ritual,* Motilal 2003

Dyczkowski, Mark *The Doctrine of Vibration - an Analysis of the Doctrines and Practices of Kashmir Shaivism* State University of New York Press 1987

Evola, Julius *The Yoga of Power: Tantra, Shakti and the Secret Way* Inner Traditions Press 1992

Feuerstein, Georg *Tantra: The Path of Ecstacy* Shambhala 1998

Feuerstein, Georg *The Yoga Sutras of Patanjali* Inner Traditions Press 1979

Feuerstein, Georg *The Yoga Tradition - its History, Literature, Philosophy and Practice* Hohm Press 2001

Flood, Gavin *The Tantric Body, The Secret Tradition of Hindu Religion* I.B. Tauris 2006

Heidgger, Martin *Contributions to Philosophy,* Indiana University Press 1999

Isaveya, Natalia *From Early Vedanta to Kashmir Shaivism,* SUNY Press 1995

Kosok, Michael *The Singularity of Awareness* Author House 2004

Lawrence, David Peter *Rediscovering God with Transcendental Argument* SUNY 1999

Malinar, Angelika *The Bhagavadgita* Cambridge 2007

Marjanovic, B. *Abhinavagupta's Commentary on the Bhagavad Gita,* Indica Books 2002

Marx, Karl *Capital: a critique of political economy* Volumes 1-3, Penguin Classics

Marx, Karl and **Engels**, Friedrich *The Communist Manifesto* Penguin Classics

Marx, Karl *Economic and Philosophical Manuscripts* Prometheus Books 1988

Mehta, J.L. *Philosophy and Religion* – Indian Council of Philosophical Research 2004

Merton, Thomas *Ghandi on Non-Violence: Selected Texts from Gandhi's "Non-Violence in Peace and War"* New Directions Paperbooks 2007

Muktananda *Nothing Exists That Is Not Shiva* SYDA Foundation 1997

Müller, Max *India: What can it teach us?* Book Tree 1999

Muller-Ortega, P.E. *The Triadic Heart of Siva* SUNY 1989

Murphy, Paul E. *Triadic Mysticism*, Motilal 1999

Pandey, K.C. *Abhinavagupta – an historical and philosophical study,* Chaukhamba 2000

Pandit, B.N. *Specific Principles of Kashmir Shaivism* Mushiram Manoharlal 1997

Perera, Jose *Hindu Theology – A Reader*, Image Books 1976

Roberts, Jane *The Seth Material* Prentice-Hall 1970

Roberts, Jane *Seth Speaks – The Eternal Validity of the Soul* Amber-Allen 1994

Singh, Jaideva *Abhinavagupta - Paratrisika-Vivarana* Motilal 2002

Singh, Jaideva *Siva Sutras – The Yoga of Supreme Identity* Motilal 2000

Singh, Jaideva *Spanda-Karikas, The Divine Creative Pulsation* Motilal 2001

Singh, Jaideva *Vijnanabhairava or Divine Consciousness* Motilal 2001

Singh, Jaideva *Pratyabehijnanahrdayam - The Secret of Self-Recognition* Motilal 2003

Swami Shankarananda *The Yoga of Kashmir Shaivism*, Motilal 2006

Urban, Hugh B. *Tantra – Sex, Secrecy, Politics and Power in the Study of Religion* University of California Press 2003

Viyogi, Naval *Nagas - The Ancient Rulers of India* D.K. Publishers 2002

Zimmer, Heinrich *Philosophies of India* ed. by Joseph Campbell, Motilal 1990

www.ingramcontent.com/pod-product-compliance
Lightning Source LLC
Chambersburg PA
CBHW060306100426
42742CB00011B/1884

Professor James Franklin is Professor of Mathematics and Statistics at the University of New South Wales. He is the author of *What Science Knows* (2009), *Life to the Full: Rights and Social Justice in Australia* (edited, Connor Court 2007), *Catholic Values and Australian Realities* (Connor Court 2006), *Corrupting the Youth: A History of Philosophy in Australia* (2003) and *The Science of Conjecture* (2001). He was awarded the 2005 Eureka Prize for Research in Ethics.

Associate Professor Greg Melleuish is an associate professor in the School of History and Politics at the University of Wollongong. He has written extensively in the area of Australian intellectual history including *Cultural Liberalism in Australia* (Cambridge University Press, 1995) and *The Power of Ideas* (Australian Scholarly Publishing, 2009). He is currently completing an intellectual portrait of James McAuley (Connor Court, forthcoming).

Dr. Philippa Martyr has been a Visiting Scholar at Oxford Brookes University, Oxford, UK and a Visiting Research Fellow at the Wellcome Unit for the History of Medicine, University of East Anglia, Norwich, UK. Her research interests include the history of medicine, mental health history, women's history, history of religion, film criticism and institutional histories.

Dr. Susanna G. Rizzo is currently a lecturer in History at Campion College Australia. She holds a BA(Hons) in Classics (specialisation: historical-religious-archaeological) from the University of Napoli 'Federico II' (Italy); a MA in International Relations; and a PhD in history from the University of Wollongong.

Dr. Sally Ninham is a long standing affiliate with La Trobe University, an independent scholar, and a published author. Until now she has relied in large part on oral history methodology to write group biography. Her first book, entitled *A Cohort of Pioneers*, was published in 2010 and her forthcoming book *Ten African Cardinals* will be published by Connor Court Publishing in 2013.

Associate Professor Paul Collits is Research Director of the University of Southern Queensland's Economic Development and Enterprise Program at its Hervey Bay campus. He has degrees in political science from the Australian National University and a PhD in geography and planning from the University of New England.

Dr. Anthony Cappello holds a PhD in History (Victoria University), MA (Arts) and a BTheo, as well as managing Connor Court Publishing. He is currently an adjunct-fellow at Ballarat University.

Professor Richard Rymarz holds the Peter and Doris Kule Chair in Catholic Religious Education at St. Joseph's College, University of Alberta, and is a Visiting Research Professor at Australian Catholic University. He has longstanding interests in religious education, youth and young adult spirituality, and the interface between Church sponsored institutions and secular culture. His latest book *The New Evangelisation* was published in 2012.

Dr. Katharine Betts is adjunct Associate Professor of Sociology at the Swinburne University of Technology. She has researched the dynamics and politics of immigration and other aspects of demography for over thirty years. She has written a number of books and articles on these topics and was co-editor of the demographic journal *People and Place* from 1993 to March 2011.